PUTTING
HUMANS FIRST

PUTTING HUMANS FIRST

Why We Are Nature's Favorite

TIBOR R. MACHAN

ROWMAN & LITTLEFIELD PUBLISHERS, INC.
Lanham • Boulder • New York • Toronto • Oxford

ROWMAN & LITTLEFIELD PUBLISHERS, INC.

Published in the United States of America
by Rowman & Littlefield Publishers, Inc.
A wholly owned subsidiary of The Rowman & Littlefield Publishing Group, Inc.
4501 Forbes Boulevard, Suite 200, Lanham, Maryland 20706
www.rowmanlittlefield.com

PO Box 317
Oxford
OX2 9RU, UK

British Library Cataloguing in Publication Information Available

Library of Congress Cataloging-in-Publication Data

Machan, Tibor R.
   Putting humans first : why we are nature's favorite / Tibor R. Machan.
      p.   cm. — (Studies in social, political, and legal philosophy)
   Includes bibliographical references and index.
   ISBN 0-7425-3345-X (hardcover : alk. paper)
   1. Human rights—Philosophy. 2. Human rights—Moral and ethical aspects.
3. Animal rights—Moral and ethical aspects. 4. Environmentalism—Moral and
ethical aspects. I. Title. II. Series.
   JC585.M4417 2004
   179'.3—dc21   2003012732

Printed in the United States of America

♾™ The paper used in this publication meets the minimum requirements of
American National Standard for Information Sciences—Permanence of Paper for
Printed Library Materials, ANSI/NISO Z39.48-1992.

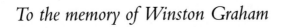

To the memory of Winston Graham

CONTENTS

ACKNOWLEDGMENTS

Some of the material in this book is reworked from essays that have been published previously, and I wish to thank the publishers for their permission to make use of them. They include the *Journal of Value Inquiry*, *Public Affairs Quarterly*, *International Journal of Social Economics*, and the *Journal des Economists et des Estudes Humaines* as well various essays I have written for newspapers and websites over the past several years.

I thank the Hoover Institution, Chapman University's Leatherby Center, and Freedom Communications, Inc., for their financial support during my preparation of this book for publication. Special thanks are due to John Raisian, Alan Bell, Dave Threshie, Dick Wallace, and Jim Doti for their ongoing encouragement of my work.

David M. Brown's and Michael Blasgen's editorial assistance has been invaluable.

I also wish to thank Nancy Gregory of the Leatherby Center for her assistance. Eve DeVaro and her staff at Rowman & Littlefield have been very supportive, as has been James P. Sterba, who has encouraged my work despite our considerable political differences.

INTRODUCTION

Tropical medicine specialist Dr. Donald Roberts and his colleagues explain in a research article that "separate analyses of data from 1993 to 1995 showed that countries that have recently discontinued their spray programs are reporting large increases in malaria incidence. Ecuador, which has increased use of DDT since 1993, is the only country reporting a large reduction (61 percent) in malaria rate since 1993."

—From "Deploy DDT to Fight Malaria," op-ed
distributed by Scripps Howard News Service, by
Angela Logomasini, June 18, 2002

Until such time as Homo sapiens should decide to rejoin nature, some of us can only hope for the right virus to come along.

—David M. Graber, in a review of Bill McKibben's
The End of Nature (from the *Los Angeles Times Book
Review*, October 22, 1989, 9)

Honorable representatives of the great saurians of older creation, may you long enjoy your lilies and rushes, and be blessed now and then with a mouthful of terror-stricken man by way of a dainty.

—John Muir, founder of the Sierra Club,
quoted in McKibben, 176

Not long ago, a television talk show featured several animal rights advocates who enjoyed considerable airtime to defend their position both analytically and emotionally.

The program exhibited little of that famous media virtue: "balance." Almost everyone, including the host, championed the animal rights position. A law professor was on hand to raise a few skeptical questions, yet even this guest provided no clearcut argument against the idea that animals enjoy rights akin to those of human beings.

One legal specialist claimed that animals must be regarded as possessing the exact same right to freedom that we assign to individual human beings. We heard how this guest had offered shelter to six dogs and were then told that this is a model that ought to be emulated throughout the world. The act was characterized as constituting a grant of asylum to the dogs—just as one might grant asylum to a political refuge from a totalitarian society.

This is also the position held by Harvard law professor Steve Wise, who has been making the rounds advocating full legal protection for at least "higher" animals like the great apes. Wise even claims to believe that these animals possess a moral nature—which, if true, would certainly give his case a fairly solid foundation inasmuch as rights are the political–legal instruments by which the moral nature of human beings is afforded scope and protection.

When the show was over, I merely filed away the experience, having already dealt with the issue of animal rights in many and various places. But then along came a National Geographic Explorer program on CNBC that in great detail depicted a polar bear's hunt for baby seals. First, we saw how the bear managed to capture and kill a baby seal. Next, we saw a mature polar bear fending off a young polar bear intent on the same seal carcass.

And then the narrator said something that was very interesting: "The older males are known to kill younger ones when fighting over carcasses."

The observation brought to mind the animal rights program of the night before and all its pat assumptions. How inconvenient that wild animals do not always behave with scrupulous decorum! No, the older bears do not share even a bit of the scavenged pickings but rather chase the young ones away or kill them outright, the better to keep everything for themselves. These greedy, violent animals seemed oblivious to the legal–moral status that had been conferred on them by the animal rights panelists just a few nights before. (Well, perhaps they don't get cable.)

Of course, human beings have slugged it out over scarce resources throughout history (although in more recent times, as the values of civilization have taken stronger root, the win–win approach of the humane economy has tended to displace the dog-eat-dog approach of violence and warfare). But in most eras and in most places, it has always been a crime to kill a young person even in defense of one's property, let alone over wild prey. And where it isn't a crime, the bulk of world opinion regards such societies as barbaric and brutal, even in this age of multiculturalism.

So, given the evident lack of moral sense of even the highest rungs in the animal world, how can we seriously entertain the idea that animals have rights like human beings do? If such rights and such moral sensibility could be imputed to them, all the brutality in the animal world would have to be construed as criminal. But, quite sensibly, it is not. Why not?

The reason is that animals, as a rule, behave as instinct dictates. In many cases, instincts dictate that the animals kill their own kind. Fish often eat their young, as do lions when impelled to do so by their genetic disposition, presumably to rid their pride of bastard offspring. Animals have no choice about how they conduct themselves, so no one can reasonably issue indictments against them, moral or legal (a practice once in force throughout Christian Europe, however). Inborn, hard-wired prompters govern their lives.

On an intuitive level, everyone understands this, even the advocates of animal rights. Yes, some scientists argue that perhaps some of the higher animals, such as great apes or orang-utans, have actually developed "culture," but this conclusion is based more on wishful—anthropomorphic—interpretation than any real evidence of culture and thought.

On the other hand, when people act brutally, we do feel justified in condemning them. Why? Why is it regarded as barbaric—and why should it be criminal—to kill children for fun, profit, or even survival if the lower animals can't rightly be blamed for violent behavior? Why indeed implore us to treat animals more humanely than some of us do?

I argue that what warrants such evaluation of human beings is that we are in fact fundamentally different from our animal kin in the wild. Why I believe this will become clear in the pages that follow.

The issues at stake are neither trivial nor academic, for they speak directly to the moral standing of human beings on this earth and how we should live our lives during the brief time we're here—whether we should be enjoying ourselves as best we can, or lashing ourselves continuously with a cat-o'-nine-tails in penitence for all the ants we stepped on today.

Sadly, environmentalists—not all of them, but all too many—seem to despise human beings and what we have wrought on this earth. They loath all the invented, artificial, "unnatural" joys that spring from human imagination and human industry. From bridges to trains and planes to coal mines and soot-producing factories, it's all a dastardly affront, a rape of nature, in their eyes. A few—a very few, we must hope— would just as soon see humans out of the picture. The previously quoted sentiment of environmentalist David Graber, who hopes for the "right virus" to come along and decimate humanity, suggests that at least some radical environmentalists must be unhappy that medical researchers have killed a few monkeys in their search for the cause of the enigmatic SARS (severe acute respiratory syndrome) virus.[1] Here we have a potentially dual affront: Animals have been killed, and humans might be saved.

It is indisputable that human activity sometimes causes environmental and other problems that must be dealt with. But it is one thing to argue for viable solutions to these problems. It is quite another to argue that humankind must leave the earth untouched altogether! I, for one, am grateful for all the despoiling. I don't want to do without air travel, word processing, or the Internet. I would have no fun—indeed, hardly any life—at all in a state of nature living off nuts and berries.

It is right for human beings to indulge in distinctively human activities. It is right to exploit nature to promote our own lives and happiness. There is no reason to feel guilt or shame about it.[2]

We are very much a part of nature—and nature is very much a part of us, too. This book argues that no animals possess rights unless they also possess a moral nature—a capacity for discerning between right and wrong and choosing between alternatives. It is this moral capacity that establishes a basis for rights, not the fact that animals, like us, have interests or can feel pain.

This work does not make a pitch for specific public policy

changes but instead explores the standards of environmental philosophy on which public policy about the environment must rest. Central to this philosophy is the view that human beings are of paramount importance when public policies and, indeed, standards of personal conduct vis-à-vis the environment are being established. Whether it is possible to direct public policy toward an environmentalism that accepts humans as first in the hierarchy of nature depends on many factors, including what people believe about the place of human beings in the natural world. It also depends on whether a sound environmentalism can be crafted when humans are indeed put first. This book proposes that the answer is yes—indeed, that a human-first environmentalism is the only kind of environmentalism worth having.

1

A CASE FOR ANIMAL RIGHTS?

Are sharks as important as little boys? Should fish or any lower animal enjoy the same moral status as human beings, along with all the rights and privileges appertaining thereto?

Among those convinced that something is terribly wrong with the expansion of human inhabitation on earth, some worry that it is human life itself that will ultimately suffer from this expansion. They believe that population control is good for people—that if there were fewer of us, those remaining would enjoy a better life. And if certain other animals are successfully preserved this, too, is good for human beings. Whether or not this view is well advised, it at least shares our common assumption that, for humans, the well-being of humans ought to be of paramount concern.

But another breed of environmentalist is not worried at all about the quality of human life. As one who has attended numerous environmental conferences, read much of the environmentalist and animal rights literature, and taken part in the scholarly debate about the issue of animal "rights" and "liberation," I know that a great many people seriously reject the idea that human beings should be the primary concern of human beings!

Some believe that it is "nature as a whole" that should be our concern and that focusing on improving human life is the evil of "speciesism." The idea is that just as it is wrong to rank a certain group of human beings over others—say, whites or the Irish over blacks or Turks—so it is wrong to rank the human species over, say, ostriches or mice or meadows. Other champions of environmental and animal causes believe that it is not so much nature that deserves our care but rather the promotion of sentient pleasure or satisfaction. These folks argue that everyone must work to increase the overall pleasure that exists in the world and that since many animals are fully capable of feeling pleasure, the improvement of their lot is every bit as important as improving the lot of humanity. Harvard legal scholar Steve Wise urges us to grant full recognition to animal rights in our legal system. Hundreds of movie stars and celebrities as well as prominent academics favor the idea of animal rights or liberation as well.[1]

These advocates of animal rights don't necessarily trumpet their views when doing so would be bad for public relations.

Consider the story of the young Florida boy Jessie Arbogast, whose arm was bitten off by a seven-foot, two-hundred-pound shark, then successfully reattached after his uncle wrestled the shark ashore and National Park Service ranger Jared Klein shot the beast dead so that the limb of the human could be retrieved from the gullet of the fish.

Few among us would have winced at this choice. To save the boy's arm, the shark had to die. But some people vehemently disagree. Yet there are thousands of animal rights advocates around the world, including sundry Hollywood celebrities and high-profile academics with easy access to the media, who in the face of this unabashed favoritism toward a human being remained completely silent about their professed view that human beings are no more important than non–human beings.

They have certainly pressed the logic of their position in other circumstances. In the American Northwest, for example, lands and waterways have been shut down by federal authorities because they might contain endangered species, a policy that is economically devastating to farmers and fishers but welcomed by animal rights advocates and environmentalists. In California, near where I live, an entire national forest is shut down and inaccessible to the public, presumably because a species of toad living there might get stepped on by visitors. Indeed, legislators have authorized various departments of the federal government to ban the human use of a wide array of forests, lakes, rivers, and parks that contain animals thought to be endangered. The government is acting on the view that any endangered species must be shielded against harm from us, so that even though these areas are supposedly public property, we may not make use of them.

When the shark was killed, however, not one rabid radical environmentalist galloped to the nearest media outlet to bray about how wrong it is to slay a fish merely to smooth the life path of a hegemonic human. Instead, they were all quieter than field mice. Why?

The major difference is this: When you attack the livelihood of people in order to try to save the wilds and its animals, that is perceived as merely opposing profit. Those who hate globalization and privatization for facilitating economic development do not hesitate in their protests because they are, after all, merely assailing greed and profit. Making a living is just a euphemism for profiteering, is it not? And since many ordinary folks at least vaguely agree that there is something unseemly about greed—and since they accept, without much skepticism, that this is what the Greens are opposing when they favor the wilds—the protesters manage to acquire a somewhat placid and unresisting audience.

If, however, it were to become clear that economic development is actually the life support of millions of human beings, especially in underdeveloped countries, and that disregarding and attacking economic development do indeed have harmful impact on human life, it would not be so easy for the radical Greens to make their pitch.

When the Florida boy lost his arm, getting it back was clearly and indisputably linked with his life, his prospects, and his future. But had his parents simply lost their livelihood—a farm and a chance to fish in a river beloved by the Greens—that would not have mattered so much to many of the people who habitually defer to the Greens on these matters. The clash between the environmental agenda and the requirements of human life are more easily perceived when blood is gushing out of a wound.

There are reasonable environmentalists who do put humans first. But there are others who don't much like human beings and who care little about how much pain their policies may bring to mere people. They're on the side of the shark, not the boy. They are savvy enough to know that if they made their position plain on each relevant occasion, they would lose their standing in the forums of civil discourse. When it is expedient to do so, they present themselves as people friendly. Their actual viewpoint, though, is one of radical egalitarianism—informed by the notion that every animal is equally important and that humans have no right to override the interests of other animals for their own purposes.

Who on earth would believe such a thing, and why?

DO ANIMALS HAVE RIGHTS?

To have a right means to be justified in preventing those who have the choice from intruding on one within a given sphere of jurisdiction. If I have the right to use a community swimming pool, no one is justified in stopping me from using the pool. When a right is considered natural, the freedom involved in having this right is justified by reference to the kind of being one is, one's nature as a certain kind of entity. The idea of natural rights was originally formulated in connection with the issue of the proper relationship between human beings, especially between citizens and governments.

Since John Locke's time, the doctrine of natural rights has weathered a turbulent intellectual history, falling into disrepute at the hands of empiricism and positivism but enjoying a revival at the hands of some influential political philosophers of the second half of the twentieth century. Ironically, at a time when natural-rights theory was beginning to lose support in the philosophical world (though still followed in law and some public policy), the idea that animals might also have rights came under increasing discussion. Most notable among those who proposed such a notion was Thomas Taylor. His anonymous work *Vindication of the Rights of Brutes*, published in 1792, discussed animal rights only in the context of disparaging human rights. More positive (though brief) was the contribution of Jeremy Bentham, who, in his *Introduction to the Principles of Morals and Legislation* (1789), argued that those animals capable of suffering are owed moral consideration. Even if those that molest us or that we wish to exploit may be killed, they may not be "tormented." Leonardo da Vinci, furthermore, reportedly said, "The day will come when men such as I will look upon the murder of animals the way they now look upon the murder of men."[2] In the latter part of the nineteenth century, Henry S. Salt devoted an entire work to the idea of animal rights.[3] And in our time, numerous philosophers and social commentators have tried to demonstrate that if we are able to ascribe basic rights to life, liberty, and property to human beings, we can do the same for many of the higher animals.

Their arguments have two essential parts. First, they subscribe to Darwin's thesis that no difference of kind, only a difference of degree, can be found between other animals and human beings.[4] Second, they claim that even if there were a difference in kind between other animals (especially mammals) and human beings, since both can be shown to have interests, for certain moral and legal purposes the difference does not matter; only the similarity matters.[5]

Advocates of animal rights defend their proposition by diverse routes. Some do so from the perspective of natural rights, treating these "rights" as basic limiting principles that may not be ignored except in circumstances when it would also make sense to disregard the rights of human beings. Even on this matter, there are serious differences among defenders of animals rights—some do not allow any special regard for human beings,[6] while some hold that when it comes to a choice between a person and a dog, it is ordinarily the person who should be given protection.[7]

Others choose to defend animal rights or obligations we owe to animals (including abstaining from hurting them) on utilitarian grounds: To the extent that it amounts to furthering overall pleasure or happiness in the world, animals must be given consideration equal to what human beings receive. Thus, an animal that is capable of experiencing pleasure or happiness may be sacrificed to further some human purpose only if that sacrifice demonstrably contributes to the overall pleasure or happiness on earth. Barring such a demonstrable contribution, animals and humans enjoy equal rights.

Natural Animal Rights

Although the idea that animals have rights goes back at least to the eighteenth century, it has only recently become a cause célèbre among numerous well-placed intellectuals, including moral and political philosophers. Jeremy Bentham, for example, seems to have suggested legislation requiring humane treatment of animals, but he did not defend animal rights per se—not surprisingly since Bentham was not impressed with the more basic (Lockean) doctrine of natural rights. Locke's idea of natural rights has had enormous influence, however. And even where Locke's specific formulation is not respected, a roughly Lockean conception of "natural rights" is often invoked as some kind of model of what it would take for a being to possess rights.

In recent years, the doctrine of animal rights has found champions in important circles where the general doctrine of rights is well regarded. For example, Professor Tom Regan, in his important book *The Case for Animal Rights*,[8] finds the idea of natural rights intellectually congenial and extends it to embrace the higher animals. The political tradition that Regan works in appears to be Lockean. But Regan does not agree that human nature is distinctive enough, in relevant respects, to restrict the scope of natural rights to humans alone.

Veganism

Some philosophers and moralists defend an allied view called veganism—a vegetarianism supposedly anchored in ethics. The English academics Les Burwood and Ros Wyeth defend this veganism. Their thesis is that no one should kill or even use animals, not even fish, because "all sentient beings are essentially similar, despite many obvious differences."

We can also describe their position as the "interest" theory of rights. On the vegan view, if you have interests, you have rights. If something can benefit from certain states, conditions, or circumstances, then it may be said to be a rights possessor. What does it have rights to? Whatever it takes to obtain that which is in its interest. Along with Bentham, John Stuart Mill is a natural forefather of the doctrine, for Mill elaborates an account of (human) rights grounded in interest. His *On Liberty*, where we get the most explicitly utilitarian if somewhat idiosyncratic theory of human rights, is the classic statement of the position. Because it is to our interest to obtain various goods, such as happiness, and because liberty is a precondition to being happy, we have a right to liberty.

We see the hazards of a purely interest-based defense of rights when we move from a political theory generally congenial to human interests to one that corrals all creatures into its ethical–political orbit. After all, all sentient beings have *interests*. "We are, each of us, the experiencing subject of a life, a conscious creature having an individual welfare that is important to us, whatever our usefulness to others," report Burwood and Wyeth. "We all want and prefer things, believe and feel things, recall and expect things. Some beings are better than others at doing these things."[9] So, clearly, "members of all sentient species have interests which should be protected and sometimes it is useful to put this in terms of their having a right to life, a right to avoid pain, a right not to be involuntarily used as a resource by others. These are core vegan beliefs."[10]

It follows that animal research, sports involving animals,

and the raising of beef, chicken, and any other animals for food are all morally wrong. All those who take part in these activities and/or accept and use their results are behaving in a morally vicious manner. Vegans insist that all such activities ought to be banned around the world. (One might also argue that plants have objective interests—to be near sunlight, soil, and water, for example—but perhaps on the vegan view it is only the consciousness of interests possible to sentient creatures that can bestow a creature with rights. Besides, if humans were not allowed to consume even veggies, even the academic-theorist population would soon expire, and that can't be right.)

Animal Liberation

Following a different tradition, that of utilitarianism, the idea of "animal liberation" has emerged. This can lead to roughly the same conclusions as those spawned by the natural-rights tradition. But for utilitarians, what is important is not that humans or other animals have a specific sphere of dominion but rather that they be well off in their lives. As long as most of the relevant creatures enjoy a reasonably high living standard, the appropriate moral and political objectives for them will have been met. But if this goal is not reached, we need to take steps to improve things. "Animal liberation" is such a step. Trashing a research laboratory and "liberating" the lab rats is one example of it.

The utilitarian and natural rights views are not so disparate. While Peter Singer does not champion animal rights per se, what he advocates is close enough to it so that partisans of Singer's theory of "animal liberation" and partisans of Regan's theory of "animal rights" have no trouble cooperating politically on behalf of animals.

WHY ANIMALS DON'T HAVE RIGHTS

The Nature of Rights

A right specifies a sphere of liberty wherein the agent has full authority to act. My *right to life* is an acknowledgment of my authority to govern my own life, to be in charge of what happens to it; my right to liberty implies my authority to take the actions I decide to take, good or bad, right or wrong, given that without this right I cannot be a morally responsible individual.

The most fundamental objection to the notion that animals have rights is the fact that only human beings have the requisite moral nature for ascribing to them basic rights. However closely humans and lower animals resemble each other, human beings alone possess the capacity for free choice and the responsibility to act ethically. Basic rights spell out the "moral space"[11] we require in our communities so as to live according to our nature as choosing, thinking, social animals. So, any principle or concept of "animal rights" rests on a category mistake—that is, the logical error of treating two different kinds of entities as equivalent in a way that they are not at all equivalent. One can understand how the mistake is made—we sympathize with animals or certain animals because of the ways they are indeed similar to us. But sympathetic extrapolation is no substitute for reasoning based on the actual, observed nature of things.

The advocates of animal rights do not want to acknowledge the implications of an inescapable fact about all the lower animals: that they live in a *wild* kingdom, which is to say they have no compunction about "abusing"—such as slaughtering and consuming—one another chronically and at will and as a matter of unimpeachable instinct.

In a review of Tom Regan's provocative book *The Case for Animal Rights*, John Hospers reports,

> As one reads page after page of Regan's book, one has the growing impression that his thesis is in an important way "going against nature." It is a fact of nature that living things have to live on other living things in order to stay alive themselves. It is a fact of nature that carnivores must consume, not plants (which they can't digest), but other sentient beings capable of intense pain and suffering, and that they can survive in no other way. It is a fact of nature that animal reproduction is such that far more creatures are born or hatched than can possibly survive. It is a fact of nature that most creatures die slow lingering tortuous deaths, and that few animals in the wild ever reach old age. It is a fact of nature that we cannot take one step in the woods without killing thousands of tiny organisms whose lives we thereby extinguish. This has been the order of nature for millions of years before man came on the scene, and has indeed been the means by which any animal species has survived to the present day; to fight it is like trying to fight an atomic bomb with a dart gun. . . . This is the world as it is, nature in the raw, unlike the animals in Disney cartoons.[12]

Now, one can dispute Hospers, but only by averting one's gaze from the facts. If animals in fact did have rights as you and I understand the concept of rights—rights that entail and mandate a hands-off policy toward other rights possessors—most of the creatures now lurking in lawns and jungles, at the very least all the carnivores, would have to be brought up on murder charges. This is what all the animal rights champions fail to heed, including Ingrid Newkirk, radical leader of People for the Ethical Treatment of Animals (PETA), who holds that it is unacceptable for us to use animals in any way at all.[13] This is why they allow themselves such vile thoughts as that "the world would be an infinitely better place without humans in it at all."[14]

If the scenario is absurd, it's so not because the concept of animal rights has been unfairly reduced to absurdity but because there is nowhere else to go. The idea of animal rights is impracticable to begin with; any attempt to visualize the denizens of the animal world benefiting from and respecting rights must collapse into fantasy willy-nilly.

The concept of rights emerged with the rise of human civilization precisely because it is needed by and applicable to human beings, given the specifically moral nature of human beings and their ambition to live with each other in mutual harmony and to mutual benefit. Rights have nothing to do with the lives of wolves and turtles because of what animal rights champions themselves admit, namely, the amoral nature of at least the bulk of the animal world.[15]

Advocates of animal rights in at least one way do admit the vast gulf between animals and humans and that humans alone are equipped to deal with moral issues. When they address us alone about these matters—when they accept all the carnage that is perpetrated by other living things, including what would be infanticide and worse if human beings were to engage in it—they clearly imply that human beings are indeed special. They imply, first and foremost, that people are indeed the only living beings capable of understanding a moral appeal. Only human beings can be implored to do right rather than wrong. Other animals just don't have the capacity for this. And so the environmentalists don't confront them with any moral arguments no matter how politically incorrect the animals may be toward one another.

And this implies that it is, after all, human beings alone

who have a moral nature and may, therefore, be regarded as the most highly developed species in nature. To admit as much explicitly would undercut all polemical avenues, however. To solve the problem, the theorists of animal rights and animal liberation typically rely on logical non sequiturs in their arguments.

Mission Incompossible

For example, contrary to Burwood and Wyeth, having interests is not a sufficient ground for having basic rights. One problem with the claim is that it violates the universalizability condition for ascribing such rights. For, clearly, some beings have an interest in benefits that others also have an interest in, so it would be impossible to respect the rights of both beings if having interests also conferred rights to the achievement of those interests.

I may well have an interest in seeing my local grocery carry a certain kind of bread. But I have no right to that bread or to compel the store to provide me with it. The United States has an interest in Kuwait's oil, perhaps, but this does not authorize it to lay claim to that oil. (This is one reason why talk about the national interest does not suffice to justify military intervention with other countries.) And while both Democratic and Republican candidates for the presidency have an interest in reaching the Oval Office, both cannot have a right to it, for only one person can be president.

Another way of putting it is that *compossibility* (mutual consistency) is a necessary feature of successful rights ascription. To ascribe to A the right to liberty implies that others akin to A in the relevant respects also get this right ascribed to them. And if the ascribed right is viable, it must be possible for rights-bearing agents to exercise it in a way that does not conflict with others' doing so as well. An interest-based theory of rights fails to satisfy this requirement because it is simply not possible for all the purportedly rights-invoking interests to be fulfilled via the specified exercise of rights. The actions such "rights" legitimate are not jointly performable.

What is true, of course, is that beings that have interests can be said to value various things in which they have an interest. Interest-bearing beings value things. And that is true about animals as well. Water, sunshine, nourishment, and various ecological conditions are all of value to animals. Clearly, however, they do not have rights just because of this (anymore than having a national interest in a foreign oil supply amounts to having a rightful claim to it).

It is important here to note that having rights imposes reciprocal obligations on others. That is what makes compossibility possible. If nonhuman animals had rights derived from their mere interests, they would have obligations to other (interest-bearing) beings. But in the animal kingdom, such a constraint is unintelligible. Zebras have an interest in and benefit from certain conditions, such as the ability to graze without being killed by a lion. But the fact that this condition is of interest or value to zebras does not imply that the lion, which also has interests (such as a clear and present interest in killing and devouring the zebra) is obligated to respect the zebra's right to roam unmolested. Moreover, in the state of nature any assertion of such obligation must be empty and pointless. The animals will just do what they're biologically programmed to do anyway.

There is nothing in the mere existence of various interests to show that human beings must respect some alleged right of zebras to keep grazing, either. What counts is not whether our exploitation of animals thwarts their interests but whether we have the right to take what is to our benefit as long as we respect the (actual rather than merely asserted) rights of others. If animals have no rights, then we may well have the right to use them for our own benefit—a right that we would not possess with respect to other human beings.

An Impractical Starting Point

Peter Singer's position falls prey to all the usual problems of utilitarianism. We cannot debate that venerable ethical tradition in full here. Still, it should be noted that nothing at all follows logically from the fact that some policies maximize and others reduce pleasure or satisfaction in the world unless it could be first demonstrated that ethics and politics consist in nothing but the maximization of aggregate satisfaction. But that is not what morality is about, at least not as most people understand morality. And fortunately so, since no one could possibly know whether any given individual action advances or reduces overall satisfaction in the world! We are morally responsible for making innumerable small-scale decisions, day in and day out. We could not make those decisions if their rightness and wrongness were determined by whether they promote or thwart overall satisfaction!

Singer has also argued that because some humans—such as retarded or senile individuals—have lower capacities than animals, it would seem that the unimpaired animal may have more rights than the impaired human inasmuch as the former has greater mental capacity and can, thus, experience pleasure or satisfaction to a greater extent than can seriously impaired human beings.

By such claims, however, Singer sets a bear trap not only

for his fellow humans but also for his own theorizing. One cannot make general claims based on special cases; one cannot even know what constitutes a special case until one first knows what constitutes a normal and typical case.

The argument for human rights rests primarily not on the particular level of intelligence or mental capacity of individual human agents but rather on their particular type of consciousness, namely, what Ayn Rand has called "volitional consciousness"; it is this form of consciousness that makes us moral agents. Only a human being completely stripped of conscious faculty—for example, an irremediably brain-dead accident victim—might be said to lack moral agency altogether. And in these cases, we do face difficult questions, such as whether to pull the plug (especially if a faint hope of recovery remains). But what can inspection of this brain-dead patient tell us about the alternatives facing a normally functioning person and how he should conduct himself? Nothing.

The principle holds true not only in moral philosophy but in every field of learning. To convey information about something, one starts by considering the thing as it exists normally, not abnormally. Suppose someone wants to learn about the Hungarian dance the czardas. It would be folly to begin by describing all the bad ways one can dance the czardas. One has no way of seeing how a botched pattern from the dance deviates from a proper pattern unless one first understands what *is* the proper pattern.

To investigate human beings and their lives, one focuses on the normal, healthy cases, not the special or exceptional ones.[16] A Martian would learn little about human beings beyond the strictly biological if he were instructed only about fetuses, infants, and the mentally ill. Nor can earthlings discover much about how to live their lives by contemplating such cases. We do need to deal with the borderline cases. But we can do so only by applying and adapting the knowledge we acquire from the normal case. We can't start with the exception and infer the rule.

Moral Patient

Tom Regan and others state that animals may not be moral agents but are indeed moral *patients*. But if you're the kind of entity that is a "moral patient," that doesn't mean you have rights thereby. A great painting by Rembrandt, a man long dead, could in this sense be a moral patient; that is, we ought to treat it in certain ways and not in others; we ought to be careful with it. But not because the painting has any rights but rather because of its great value for us as a work of art and also because of the wider respect for culture that informs our actions generally as civilized human beings. The same goes for Indian burial grounds as well as many artifacts and historical treasures. None has rights, but all can be moral patients—if by this we mean nothing more than that human beings can have moral responsibilities with respect to them.

Concern for Nature

Some opponents of human use of animals bypass all the stuff about interests and net satisfaction and simply insist that all life is sacred and therefore we may not intrude on any of it. Yet without killing some animals, we cannot live at all. We would squander our own lives by adhering to such a principle. Others insist that it is nature, as it stands apart from human beings, that's sacred so that disturbing it is morally wrong and should be legally wrong, too.

This broader principle would ban from human use every-thing from redwoods to caribou. But again, it is a mere asser-tion. How could nature be sacred? Who blessed it, and why weren't we human beings blessed in the same sanctifying ges-ture—a blessing that would render our way of life, the one that constantly involves our exploitation of nature, blessed as well?

There are times when we can make a plausible argument for banning the use of nature and other animals—but only when such use jeopardizes human beings or interferes with their rights. Self-defense and the requirements of human flour-ishing are good reasons for leaving alone certain parts of nature, to be cultivated or guarded against abuse. But the application of this criterion must be left to human discretion, the discretion of the owner in each case, since no humans have moral author-ity to dictate to other humans how to act unless they are being attacked by them (that is, unless their rights are being in-fringed). Sometimes it does happen that attacking some realm of nature will ipso facto mean attacking human beings as well. The victims of the assault may then defend themselves and whichever parts of nature (for example, livestock, pets, lands, forests, and so forth) belong to them.

In any case, banning the human use of animals can be ac-complished justly only if due process is followed, which means putting those who are charged with doing violence to us or our land or livestock on trial and proving the case against them in a court of law—not by just handing down special-interest legis-lation to that end.

Concern for Animals

For some people, the only thing about this subject they are sure of is that it distresses them to think of animals feeling pain or fear or grief. And it seems to them that without ascribing rights to animals, treating animals in ways that gratuitously induce pain, fear, or grief cannot be adequately discouraged.

No doubt many animals are miserable at times, often because humans make them so. Of course, this alone implies nothing as far as any rights are concerned. People, too, are often miserable without anyone having violated their rights. Sometimes even when others are responsible, no rights violations need have occurred. Consider lovers who betray each other or athletes who injure their opponents or sparring partners in contact sports. So even in the context of human interactions, bad things done by one person to another do not always involve violations of rights.

Some might argue that if we have moral tasks that the lower animals don't have, this might, admittedly, be a reason why we have rights that *supersede* theirs. But, they would argue, couldn't the logic of the argument for human rights be used to show that animals (and even plants) have rights as long as their rights don't interfere with those of beings that are more important? For example, animals might have some rights to property because, as human rights theory proposes, "to flourish as the beings they are," they need part of earth to be preserved as their natural habitat. And, of course, they would also need to be alive and free to flourish. Moreover, the killing and suffering inflicted by nonhuman animals on other nonhuman animals is necessary for their survival qua the kind of animals they are. Human beings, however, do much of such infliction of suffering for sport and convenience, not out of necessity.

First, it is not at all established that all the killing and infliction of suffering done in the nonhuman animal world is necessary for survival. When some lions kill the cubs in their pride, it is not at all clear that they are driven to do this by vital evolutionary forces. It does seem evident that the cat plays with the mouse as it prepares to kill it.

Second, just what is necessary for human life is not made clear by this objection. Arguably, human beings are the sort of animals whose flourishing requires more than bare survival. All the achievements in the arts, philosophy, athletics, and so forth attest to this. Mere survival is not *human* survival. If, perchance, the development of some human potentialities requires the use of animals, even inflicting suffering on them, that may well be exactly what makes such use morally proper and unobjectionable.

As one drives to the theater, for instance, one may crush many small and even not-so-small nonhuman animals, causing pain and suffering. It would not be a human life that did without such activities as going to the theater once in a while. Yet doing so will normally do some damage to certain animals.

The sentiments of sympathy for animals are powerful and have certainly helped engender a widespread movement in favor of ascribing rights to animals. If there were no other way to address this concern for animals, one might be tempted to conclude that the normative conceptual framework of basic rights to life, liberty, and property would need to be stretched to encompass a notion of animal rights. Any contention that ethical concerns never arise with respect to treatment of animals is just too obviously off base to be convincing. While our intuitions may not suffice to make complete sense of the moral landscape involved here, they do justify being attentive to an area of our lives where they are so powerful. To claim, for example, that it is irrelevant whether one tortures an animal, abuses it, or even lets it starve under normal circumstances would seem to contradict too much of our lives to let it go. So clearly there is need for a moral analysis of this realm of human conduct.

Is it wrong to use animals for certain nonvital purposes? Quite likely, ethically, but this is not the same conclusion as holding that animals have rights. One advocate of animal rights begins his argument with the rather mild point that "reason requires that other animals are as much within the scope of moral concern as are men" but then hops to the more radical claim that we must therefore "view our entire history as well as all aspects of our daily lives from a new perspective."[17] But the concept of rights simply cannot be appropriated as a rationale for the humane treatment of animals without corrupting it and rendering it untenable for human use, that is, for politics and law.

On the other hand, the issue of rights does not exhaust the field of morality. Human morality, including as it relates to animals, arises in connection with the practice of various major and minor virtues, including generosity, temperance, and moderation. One would damage one's character by being cruel, wasteful, or callous toward animals, given that they can experience pain, which is certainly a bad thing for them. This insight is recognized in our commonsense attitudes as we help shape our children's sensibilities toward animals. One need have no such concept as animal rights in mind to object to a child's torture of animals. Think about our disapproval of boys who pull the legs off flies. Growing up on a farm in Hungary, I received all kinds of admonition about how I ought to treat the animals. I was scolded for mistreating a cat but earned approval for taking the favorite cow grazing every day and establishing some kind of bond with it. Hardly anyone can have escaped one or another moral lecture from parents or neighbors concerning the proper treatment of cats, dogs, or birds.

I recall that when a young boy tried out his air gun by shooting a pigeon near his home, he suffered no end of tongue-lashing as a result. Yet those who rebuked the boy were not implying that "we must view our entire history as well as all aspects of our daily lives from a new perspective." Rather, they seemed to understand that reckless disregard for the life or well-being of animals shows a defect of character, a lack of sensitivity, a certain callousness. Such an assessment is completely consistent with the belief that numerous human purposes justify our routine exploitation of animals. The suffering of animals is of concern to all conscientious human beings—but not to the point of sacrificing significant human benefits to spare animals the degree of suffering needed to secure those benefits.[18]

Human beings have rights because of our moral nature. Clear delineation and respect for our rights enables us to lead our lives as we choose, well or badly, without having others impose another way of life on us. But for creatures that lack this capacity and will never develop it, rights are moot. They make no choices for which they must take responsibility. So while it may be cruel and inhumane to treat your pet poodle badly as a matter of caprice, it's not because his rights are being violated thereby.

Should there, nevertheless, be laws against certain kinds of cruelty to animals? This is not something I am willing to address fully here. Suffice it to say that, for my part, I would not necessarily take exception if someone were to rescue an animal being treated with cruelty, even if this amounted to invading someone's private property. If one spotted a neighbor torturing his cat, albeit on his own private property, one could well be morally remiss in failing to invade the place and rescue the animal. A court might correctly consider this to be illegal trespassing but still pardon the transgressor as a matter of judicial discretion. Exactly where this leaves us with the matter of whether laws should exist to ban cruelty to animals I am not sure.

But I am sure that politics ought not be a solution of first resort for many of the moral issues that confront us. Sadly, though, in our day most moral issues are indeed dealt with by political means, almost by default, even when voluntary means are available. Those who genuinely care for animals should consider the possibility that to the extent arguments for animal rights succeed, they may only confer additional power on governments and bureaucrats to run our lives for us. And this confiscation of responsibility may well reduce the impetus for ordinary laypersons to explore seriously how they ought to treat animals! For once an issue is relegated to the government for treatment, the civilian population tends to become complacent about it, figuring it is now taken care of without any initiative on their own part. (Most of us, for example, do not take active part in crime control—that is deemed, in this case rightly, I think, the job of specialists.)[19]

The Wrong Rights

A paradox of much contemporary talk of rights in academia is that dogmatic certainty is so often juxtaposed with shoulder-shrugging skepticism. Even as fewer and fewer academics support individual *human* rights to life, liberty, and property—in part because they regard them as unjustifiably universalistic—more and more are championing the same rights for animals. The skepticism—often resting on the view that because different communities may make different principles applicable to their inhabitants, no universal system of political principles can be made applicable to all persons—seems not to apply to the animal rights thesis. (Perhaps the most articulate and vociferous champion of this skeptical view on human rights is Richard Rorty, who explicitly dismisses them but in none of his works disputes the existence of animal rights.[20]) At the same time, however, the cause of universal rights for animals is gaining a strong following within the philosophical community. That alone is a provocative inconsistency. But it would make logical sense on at least one level: if the insistence on animal rights were a ploy for undermining real human rights.

We can sweep such contradictions aside, however, if we establish that human beings do indeed have rights—universal rights—derived from a specifically rational, moral nature that the lower animals obviously lack.

Then we can put humans first with a clear conscience. Kill the shark, let the boy live.

2

THE CASE FOR SPECIESISM

I am a "speciesist." I admit it!

By this awkward neologism, I mean pretty much what the animal liberationists mean by it (minus the negative connotation): that I elevate human beings above all other species. Not only do I consider the human animal to be in fundamental respects superior to all other animals, I also regard human beings as the very most important kind of animal—certainly the most important to ourselves.

But unlike my philosophical opponents on this question, I do not regard "speciesism" to be an arbitrary prejudice. It is grounded, rather, in certain facts of nature, including the facts of human nature. Far from being morally suspect, for human beings to practice "speciesism" is morally mandatory—if happiness and success in life are worthwhile human pursuits.

THE CIRCLE OF LIFE

We find a poetic statement of the opposite view in the autobiography of Albert Schweitzer, wherein he reports that the sacredness of life, all life, struck him with the force of an epiphany during a ride on an African river. He was, he recalls, "struggling to find the elementary and universal conception of the ethical which I had not discovered in any philosophy. Sheet after sheet I covered with disconnected sentences, merely to keep myself concentrated on the problem. Late on the third day, at the very moment when, at sunset, we were making our way through a herd of hippopotamuses, there flashed upon my mind, unforeseen and unsought, the phrase, 'Reverence for Life.' The iron door had yielded; the path in the thicket had become 'visible.'"[1]

What does this reverence imply? For Schweitzer, that "I must interpret the life around me as I interpret the life that is my own. My life is full of meaning to me. The life around me must be full of significance to itself. If I am to expect others to respect my life, then I must respect the other life I see, however strange it may be to mine."[2]

This egalitarian obligation implies that one must never injure or destroy other life—*any* life—unless it is deemed "necessary" to do so. But this escape hatch is a booby trap: "Whenever I injure any kind of life I must be quite certain that it is necessary. I must never go beyond the unavoidable, not even in apparently insignificant things. The farmer who has mowed down a thousand flowers in his meadow in order to feed his cows must be careful on his way home not to strike the head off a single flower by the side of the road in idle amusement, for he thereby infringes the law of life without being under the pressure of necessity."[3]

Schweitzer's ethic seems both stricter and more lenient than those who limit their strictures to the higher animals. He at least recognizes that humanity, to survive, must make "necessary" use of nature. On the other hand, a properly respectful human must, in his view, be on tiptoe around *all* living organisms, from gnats to dandelions. Yet in practice, Schweitzer's differences with other environmentalist egalitarians are fairly minor. The result must be continuous apprehension and guilt. Can a person live his life with anything other than timorous Naderite caution if he must worry about every casually obliterated instance of inferior life, whether the threat to one's moral purity manifests itself in the form of crushed dandelions or pulverized squirrels?

The "reverence for life" ethic becomes problematic as soon as one tries to conscientiously live by it. For example, what does "necessary" injury to nonhuman life even mean here? If the farmer has sinned by plucking a dandelion in a moment of idle amusement, is he really any the less culpable for mowing them down en masse to feed a herd of animals all of which he intends to kill later on? How about plucking a rose to give to his girl? What could make breaching the "law of life" justifiable in the one instance but not in the other? Does the "law of life" trump human needs and purposes or vice versa? On this view, how intense and immediate must a need be before one is allowed to destroy other life to fulfill it?

Schweitzer's law of life is supposed to govern human conduct without being either informed by or subordinated to human purposes. But there is no way for humans to in fact avoid damaging other life as demanded by egalitarian sentiment and still survive, hence the tacked-on exception granted by the demands of "necessity." But "necessity" cannot serve as a criterion for amending the "law of life" without reference to specifically human purposes and values—and these human purposes cannot be discussed without reference to what distinguishes human life from dandelion life. But once one grants that there are such distinctions, one can no longer be justified in "interpret[ing] the life around me as I interpret the life that is my own."

And Schweitzer's ethic isn't even intelligible when one focuses only on the similarities between human life and other forms of life. For what kind of "reverence for life" neglects the fact that all organisms without exception, not just humans, destroy and feed on other life chronically and as a matter of course? Such quandaries and contradictions can't be swept away by the exhilaration of mystic epiphanies, however deeply felt.

REVERENCE FOR LIFE?

Reverence is the feeling one experiences when one very much admires or prizes something. Indeed, if something is worthy of reverence, it is usually supreme in worth or value. Is, then, life—all life, indiscriminately—worthy of our reverence? Are we justified in revering all life, as if it were all on the same level as "the life that is my own"?

It is only human beings, at least as far as we now know, who can revere. If there is to be a "law of life" that stands above and apart from nature as it presents itself to us, it is only human beings who can formulate and respect it. Only human beings have the capacity to understand the worth of something and thus can give homage to this understanding by revering what they understand to be of great worth.

Life is a process—an internal, ultimately self-generated process—of keeping something functioning as a certain kind of entity. "Life" as such is an abstract concept used to designate all things that live. Since there are many different kinds of living beings, it is not possible to think about life without considering that it is the life of some sort of being—some particular plant or animal.

If one asks whether life is to be revered, one must know what sort of life is at issue. Are we speaking of ants, cockroaches, viruses, bacteria, cats, dogs, horses, or human beings? Are we speaking of life at any stage of its development, in any of its manifestations, whether diseased or malformed, healthy or flourishing, free or confined?

The short answer is no. We cannot revere all life indiscriminately. Life in general includes innumerable manifestations, some good, some bad, some mediocre. Some life should not be revered—the life of dangerous or disease-carrying entities, for example. How can we revere that which destroys us? We could do so only if reverence as a human emotion and response were disconnected somehow from the impact on our own lives. But this would mean we weren't revering our *own* lives very much at all!

We must acknowledge there is a hierarchy within the class of living beings, such that some living things are of lower quality, others of higher. An ant is less developed, less complex, less capable of creativity and variety of experience than is a dog or, especially, a human being. Thus, we are speaking not only of many different lives but also of lives of different qualities. An ethic of egalitarian reverence attempts to blur such differences, but they exist just the same.

VALUES IN NATURE

An objective understanding of nature cannot justify an indiscriminate "reverence for life." But it can justify a certain type of anthropocentrism or speciesism—that is, the view that human beings are more important or valuable than other aspects of nature, including plants and animals.

A few clarifications. First, by "more important or valuable," I do not mean any such estimation as determined by a mythical, utterly disinterested observer, existing somehow outside nature, who is antiseptically ranking the values of elements of nature "in themselves." Something is important or valuable when it makes a positive or advantageous difference to something or someone—as when we say that the sun is important for the plant or that his home is a value to John. The relational nature of value becomes clear when we attempt to trace the implications of a principle of "reverence for life" that is purportedly established without reference to human concerns. Human beings cannot step outside themselves in making judgments of value. But the agent-relative nature of values is no objection to making such judgments either, as long as the human agent's necessarily human perspective is informed by nature as it really is rather than nature as reconstituted by poetry or ideology. We need to make such judgments in order to survive!

Second, by anthropocentrism, I do not mean that human beings—as a collectivity—are the *telos* of existence, that is, the ultimate aim or end or the central fact of the universe, only that human beings are of the highest value in the known universe.

Third, by human beings, I mean individual human beings—you, me, Joe, Mary, and so forth. Individuals are not isolated "atoms," but neither are they merely a subordinate unit of a collective whole.[4] There is no concrete universal "human being," only individual, particular human beings with particular lives and goals.

The conception of humanity as a kind of collective entity derives, in the main, from the legacy of Platonic metaphysics that, at least in its standard rendition, regards general abstract ideas or universals as concrete albeit intellectual or spiritual beings—the "Forms" of which the individual entities we see around us are said to be but pale reflections. Such a view—that abstractions exist somehow outside the mind, as templates—is metaphysically unsound. On the other hand, individuals do share commonalities with other individuals. They are of a specific kind, such as human, feline, male, apple, and so forth. For anthropocentrism to be metaphysically cogent, individual human beings would have to be the class of beings that are the most valuable (to us) in nature.

This concept of individualist anthropocentrism should preempt any objections grounded on the philosophical and moral weaknesses of what we might call "radical individualism," the sort of individualism derived from Thomas Hobbes and carried to its logical conclusion by the nineteenth-century German social thinker Max Stirner. The individualism or egoism discussed here—dubbed "classical," so as to distinguish it from the "atomic" or "radical" variety commonly criticized by those who stress the social nature of human beings—recognizes that the human individual is so classified for good reasons, based on the rational recognition of kinds of beings in nature. This view would justify not only personal but also various social virtues—generosity, charity, and compassion.

Here a point needs to be raised concerning the perfectly sensible Aristotelian understanding of human beings as essentially social animals. Ecologists tend to stress this point often when individualism is presented to them as a sociopolitical alternative to their widely embraced collectivism (whether in a socialist, welfare statist, or communitarian version).

Being essentially an individual does not preclude an essential social dimension to one's life. Given that an individual life

has much to benefit from social involvement, it is "in one's nature" to be social as well as a matter of one's individual decision
to embark on a rich social, community, and political life. It may
well be one's moral responsibility as an individual to connect
with other human beings—unless, of course, the available others are real dangers to one's life, which in the case of human
beings is a clear possibility.

Individualist anthropocentrism also recognizes that a moral
virtue, to *be* such a virtue, must be practiced by choice and cannot be coerced. While recognizing the social dimension of life,
the position here considered is still a bona fide individualism
in that it identifies human nature as essentially individual—in
contrast to, for example, Karl Marx, for whom "the human es-
sence is the true collectivity of man"[5]; or August Comte, according to whom the social point of view "cannot tolerate the
notion of rights, for such notion rests on individualism. We are
born under a load of obligations of every kind, to our predeces-
sors, to our successors, to our contemporaries. . . . [Man must
serve] Humanity, whose we are entirely."[6]

If my own argument is sound, it will indicate why, in discussing environmental ethics—whether at the level of principles or of applied morality—the highest value must be
attributed to measures that enhance the lives of individual
human beings on earth. The aim is to defend the anthropocentric position from within a naturalistic framework—that is, on
the basis of our understanding of the natural world, including
the nature of living beings such as plants, animals, and human
beings.[7]

How do we establish that human beings are the most important or valuable species in nature? By considering whether
the idea of lesser or greater importance or value in the nature
of things makes clear sense and applying it to an understanding

of whether human beings or other animals are more important. If it turns out that ranking things in nature as more or less important makes sense and if humans qualify as more important than other animals, there is at least the beginning of a reason why we may make use of other animals for our purposes—for instance, when a trade-off is unavoidable.

That there are things of different degree of value in nature is admitted by animal rights advocates and environmentalists themselves, so there is no need to argue about that here. When they insist that we treat animals differently from the way we treat, say, rocks—so that we may use rocks in ways that we may not use animals—such champions testify, at least by implication, that animals are more important than rocks. They happen, also, to deny that human beings rank higher than other animals, or at least they do not admit that ranking human beings higher warrants our using animals for our purposes. But that is a distinct issue. What matters for now is that variable importance in nature is at least implicitly admitted by defenders of the high moral status of animals.

In any case, there simply is evidence through the natural world of the existence of beings of greater complexity *and* of higher value. For example, while it makes no sense to evaluate as good or bad such things as planets or rocks or pebbles— except as they may relate to human or other living beings— when it comes to plants and animals, the process of evaluation commences very naturally indeed. We can speak of better or worse oaks, redwoods, zebras, foxes, or chimps.

For such beings, we confine our evaluation to the condition or behavior without any intimation of their responsibility for being better or worse. But when we start discussing human beings, our evaluation assumes a moral component. To the best of our knowledge, it is with human beings that moral responsibility enters the universe.

Clearly, a hierarchical structure in nature is thus exhibited. There is evidence throughout the natural world of lesser and greater complexity as well as lesser and greater capacity to value (and, at a certain point in biological development, be appropriately subject to evaluation by other organisms capable of such assessment). Some things—rocks, comets, and minerals—do not invite evaluations at all and have no capability of any kind of "valuing"—a capacity specific to living entities. When we look at the living world, we find, broadly speaking, two kinds of valuing entities. Some organisms—zebras, frogs, and redwoods—pursue goals related to their survival that are wired into their natures and thus invite evaluation as to whether they do well or badly but without any moral or ethical implications. And some organisms—human beings—invite *moral* evaluation in light of the fact that they exercise choice regarding the good and bad things they can do.

Normal human life involves moral tasks, and that is why we are more important than other beings in nature. We are subject to moral appraisal; it is largely a matter of our own doing whether we succeed or fail in our lives. Clearly, if we could not make such comparative evaluations rationally, there would be little point to environmental ethics in the first place, a field that presupposes value differentiation throughout the natural world.

Now, when it comes to our moral task, namely, to succeed as human beings, we must try to reach sensible conclusions about what we should do. We can fail to do this—and too often do so. But we can also succeed. The process that leads to our success involves learning, among other things, what it is that nature avails us with to achieve our highly varied tasks in life.

Clearly, among these highly varied tasks could be some

that make judicious use of animals—for example, to find out whether some medicine is safe for human use, we might wish to employ animals. It is rational for us to make the best use possible of nature in order to succeed in living our lives. That does not mean that we can do without guidelines for how we might make use of animals—any more than we can do without guidelines for any aspect of our conduct. Such guidelines are essential in the field of ethics. But they are not the proper subject of politics or law in a free society (except insofar as animals or plants become the subject of contractual agreements and their enforcement).

The previous line of reasoning counters a frequently raised objection to our use of other animals: Could not the same argument be used within the human species, giving better people the right to make use of "worse" people? The answer is that making choices is a precondition for determining who is better or worse among human beings, and using people against their will squelches their choice. So those who are better have the obligation to leave those who are worse to continue to make choices that may well improve their situation. We are free to use the lower animals not because they are less capable than us of playing chess or maintaining friendships but because they lack our moral faculty altogether. This is not true of other human beings, whatever their shortcomings may be.

Of course, we do in fact "make use" of some very bad people—those who have been duly convicted of having violated the reasonable requirements of human community life. We banish—usually by imprisonment—those who violate the basic rights of others. Personally, too, there are limits to tolerance: If someone threatens us with serious harm, with taking our lives or property, we act to subdue the aggressor and end the threat. Such actions do not constitute "using" someone per se, of course; they are defensive rather than exploitative. But such examples do show that for self-defensive purposes, human beings can be justified in killing or maiming other beings, just as we might treat animals if they stand in the way of our flourishing.

Why is a rational being more valuable to us than animals that lack conceptual and moral capacity? Why would the emergence of a moral dimension—one that involves the choosing capacity of the agent—elevate the being with such agency in the eyes of any reasonable evaluator?

For one thing, beings that lack a rational faculty also lack the capacity to contribute creatively to the values in nature. By contrast, human beings *can* create value, as a matter of our own initiative, not merely exhibit it. We can produce a culture of science, art, athletics, and so forth, the diverse features of which can themselves be valued. This enables human beings, for example, to replace some lost values in nature if that turns out to be the right course for them to take. So the emergence of choice—the moral component—clearly makes a valuable difference. It's value-adding, as it were.

Some might object that simply because human beings are capable of moral responsibility, it does not follow that they are the only beings of moral worth. But we need to keep in mind that to ascribe moral worth or merit to something or to deny that it has such worth or merit entails relating it to human action from the outset. A wonderful sunny day has no moral worth, nor does a destructive earthquake suffer from moral deficit. (If we imagine such occurrences on a barren rock of a planet, as opposed to our own inhabited one, the point is especially evident. A wonderful sunny day cannot be good for anyone, let alone revered by anyone, when no one is around to experience it.)

Morality pertains to the capacity to make choices among real alternatives. So something can have moral worth or lack it only if some human (or other rational, choosing) agent produces or destroys it. Thus, the success of a symphony may have moral worth, just as the failure of a savings-and-loan association may lack it (or even have moral disvalue). Men and women who produce morally good actions and results are considered to be morally worthwhile for that reason. But we do not regard horses or tidal waves as either morally good or morally evil. Human agency is the sine qua non of moral worth.

Some might ask whether creating what *has* value is the same thing as *creating* value. But these conceptualizations differ only with respect to level of generality. X's having value (that is, having a positive effect on something else) is, more broadly characterized, the phenomenon of value per se in nature. Things cannot be values in a void without being pleasing to or enhancing of or supportive of something else in some specific way. We may even say that *value is a type of fact* in relation to living beings that face the alternative between flourishing and decaying, living or dying. Broadly speaking, what is of value contributes to life, and what is of disvalue leads to death.[8]

THE IMPORTANCE OF BEING HUMAN

Of course, even if it were not the case that human beings are more valuable than other aspects of nature, it is doubtful any conclusions could follow from this that would warrant policies awarding priority to these other aspects of nature. Only if it could be shown that beings other than humans do qualify as supremely important—based on arguments that draw not on esoteric knowledge or intuition but on commonly accessible evidence and sound theories—might we be obliged to yield our policies focusing primarily on human welfare in favor of some more comprehensive objective.[9]

So far, there is no clear evidence that any species other than human beings reside at the top of the natural hierarchy. When human beings emerge in the natural world, so does the capacity to think and exercise self-initiative. That is why Aristotle calls us "the rational animal."

To be sure, some people—infants and certain invalids—cannot be characterized as fully responsible moral agents. There are some who have become so ill or incapacitated that we excuse their conduct even when they act in ways we would normally consider reprehensible. But these are exceptions, explained by reference to the special conditions of debilitation or disease.

That the lower animals do not qualify as rational beings is something we know not from a syllogistic proof but from reflecting on the evidence. We never observe them operating in a cognitively productive manner. For example, no animal raises the question of whether animals are thinking beings nor makes any television programs on the subject. Animals, furthermore, have no central, crucial need of thinking, whereas human beings cannot begin to survive without thinking. And unlike animals, human beings cannot count on instincts to guide them automatically. For those lower animals that do exhibit some rudimentary cognitive capacity, it is very much a side issue, elicited usually by human beings in highly circumscribed and unusual circumstances (such as laboratories).

Even so, some argue that a measure of morality can indeed be found within the world of at least higher animals, such as dogs. Bernard Rollin maintains that it is impossible to clearly distinguish between human and nonhuman animals, including on the grounds of moral agency. He holds that "in actual fact, some animals even seem to exhibit behavior that bespeaks something like moral agency or moral agreement."[10] His argument for this is rather anecdotal, but it is worth considering:

> Canids, including the domesticated dog, do not attack another when the vanquished bares [*sic*] its teeth, showing a sign of submission. Animals typically do not prey upon members of their own species. Elephants and porpoises will and do feed injured members of their species. Porpoises will help humans, even at risk to themselves. Some animals will adopt orphaned young of other species. (Such cross-species "'morality'" would certainly not be explainable by simple appeal to mechanical evolution, since there is no advantage whatever to one's own species.) Dogs will act "'guilty'" when they break a rule such as one against stealing food from a table and will, for the most part, learn not to take it.[11]

Animal rights advocates such as Rollin maintain that it is impossible to clearly distinguish between human and nonhuman animals, including on the grounds of moral agency. Yet what they do to defend this point is to invoke borderline cases, imaginary hypotheses, and anecdotes.

In contrast, in his book *The Difference of Man and the Difference It Makes*, Mortimer Adler undertakes the painstaking task of showing that even with full acknowledgment of the merits of Darwinian and, especially, post-Darwinian evolutionary theory, there is ample reason to uphold the doctrine of species distinction—a distinction, incidentally, that is actually presupposed within Darwin's own work.[12] Adler shows that although the theistic doctrine of radical species differences is incompatible with current evolutionary theory, the more naturalistic view that species are superficially (but not negligibly) different is indeed necessary to the theory. The fact of occasional border-line cases is simply irrelevant to the *normal* case—what is crucial is the generalization that human beings are basically different from other animals by virtue of "a crucial threshold in a continuum of degrees."[13] As Adler explains,

> Distinct species are genetically isolated populations between which interbreeding is impossible, arising (except in the case of polyploidy) from varieties between which interbreeding was not impossible, but between which it was prevented. Modern theorists, with more assurance than Darwin could manage, treat distinct species as natural kinds, not as man-made class distinctions. . . .[14]
>
> Without the critical insight provided by the distinction between superficial and radical differences in kind, biologists [as well as animal rights advocates, one should add] might be tempted to follow Darwin in thinking that all differences in kind must be apparent, not real.[15]

However controversial the status of certain almost-but-not-quite-cognitive animals like chimpanzees or dolphins,[16] you might think that the existence of moral agency could not be seriously disputed when it comes to human beings themselves. Yet in the history of philosophy, human nature has indeed been the subject of serious and fundamental controversy. Such clashes have import not only with respect to how human beings ought to conduct themselves generally (and even whether it makes sense to issue moral advice) but also with respect to how we ought to treat the environment. Environmentalism is, after all, a moral undertaking and a matter of choice—unless, of course, the natural world is completely deterministic and human beings have no choice about their place in it at all.

These are live issues. Perhaps the most problematic aspect of a philosophical reflection on environmental issues is that two incommensurable approaches to the world here meet head-on. On the one hand, ecology is a natural science, and the developments in the natural world bearing on that science are often deemed to be a matter of ineluctable laws. Whether some forest is sturdy or vulnerable is, thus, thought to be a matter not of human choice but of how life evolved here on earth. On the other hand, in public policy debates, we constantly raise questions about how we ought to act vis-à-vis the natural world—whether we ought to release or not release various chemicals into the air, cut down forests, engage in strip mining, preserve some animal species, and so forth.

Yet if evolutionary forces drive earth's ecological system in an entirely deterministic way—including human interaction within that system—then there is no room for free choice in how we comport ourselves vis-à-vis the rest of the environment. This means trouble for any claim that human beings are moral agents, that they ought to have done this and not that, or that they should carry on, henceforth, this rather than that way! If, however, we indeed ought to do one thing rather than another vis-à-vis our environment—if an actual alternative does confront us rather than a predetermined and unavoidable course—then impersonal evolutionary forces *do not* drive the development of nature, at least not all of it—human will or choice has a role, too.

So we cannot ignore the issue of just what human nature is as we consider what kind of environmental approach needs to be taken to deal with that part of human life optimally. And these issues are closely connected to broader metaphysical issues about causality, free will, and individuality.

THE PROBLEM OF NORMS

For centuries, at least since the time of Thomas Hobbes in philosophy and Galileo in science, the notion that human beings can choose how they act has been a bone of contention. Indeed, this has always been a focus of controversy among philosophers and others interested in the nature of human life. Hobbes spent his life disputing the idea of free will, claiming that a proper understanding of the laws of nature renders the idea nonsense. Freedom, rather, is to be understood not as the human capacity to take the initiative, to cause things to happen in the world, but solely as the absence of intrusiveness on one's behavior from other persons—political freedom, in other words.

Today there are numerous champions of just this view: No such idea as free will is compatible with what science tells us about ourselves, except insofar as we mean by it that people aren't being made to do what they do but do it without interference. Any other notion of free will, it's argued, flies in the face of the findings of the natural and social sciences, which tell us that there are in our case, as in the case of any other beings in the universe, laws of nature that govern how we behave. (The most explicit, no-holds-barred advocate of this view was the late B. F. Skinner.)

If this view is correct, then there is a serious problem about any talk of how human beings ought to act. As Kant taught us, the concept "ought" implies the concept "can," so that if one ought to act so and so, one would have to have the capacity to choose either to act that way or not to do so. And that is how we see normative concerns in our personal and public affairs: If you ought to make your bed, it is up to you whether you do it—you have to have that choice. If, however, you do not have that choice, if it is not up to you whether you make or not make the bed, then to hold you responsible to make it is out of court. And if you ought not to murder, rape, or kidnap someone, you would have to be free to make the choice between doing or not doing so.

Morality and law assume human initiative, free will, causal agency. They stand against the idea that all of what we do is caused by previous events impinging on us, causing us to behave and move as we do.

Often when even the most intelligent folks speak about evolution, they tend to assume that if such a process is how human beings emerged in this world, it must be a fatalistic sort of system. Whatever happened had to happen, and whatever didn't just couldn't have happened. In other words, impersonal determinism and evolution often go hand in hand for a lot of folks.[17]

There really is no justification for this idea. If the evolutionary process could produce swimming, flying, or crawling things, why could it not also produce thinking things who must generate their own survival and thrive largely by their own initiative? Why couldn't the evolutionary process produce an organism that possesses free will?

There is no reason it couldn't, provided that free will is understood as a natural capacity rather than as some kind of inexplicable, supernatural one.

What if having free will means no more than that whoever has it can start to do things without having to be impelled to do them? Surely there is nothing unnatural about human initiative unless one builds into one's idea of nature a feature of ineluctable determinism that may or may not be there, which may indeed be present in some circumstances but not in others. It is not scientific to come at the issue of human agency with prejudice, assuming that nature cannot manifest such agency. What if it can? Such, then, would be nature. We should derive our idea of nature from studying nature—not by writing a pseudo-philosophical script mandating what nature must be like, then interpreting what we see in light of the script.[18]

Morality, too, could well emerge within the course of nature's development. With the kind of life that human beings live, one in which they need to make various original moves, they face the question of what to do. And they need standards by which to distinguish right and wrong conduct.

Not Even a Soft Billiard Ball

As a normative enterprise, environmentalism assumes that we are, indeed, free to choose some of what we do. That capacity is implicit in admonishing people to do the right thing vis-à-vis various environmental issues. Blaming a firm for polluting the environment makes no sense if that is what had to happen, just as it makes no sense to blame a meteor that hits a farmhouse or a tornado that demolishes a trailer park. The underlying view of human nature of normative environmentalism is that in the case of human beings, some attribute exists that makes it possible to make free choices that are open to critical assessment. We ought to save fuel, reduce the production of chlorofluorocarbons, stop rain forest destruction, cut down on air pollution, and so forth. Such injunctions are meaningless unless we are free to make choices as to how we act.

But what does this view of human nature assume? For one,

that normal people can of their own initiative start to do some things or, alternatively, fail to start to do it. Such is suggested by the ordinary expression "Damn it, I didn't think" when a person makes a mistake. Indeed, it is with thinking (or the lack of it) that human actions generally get started—which makes sense given the fact that what distinguishes us from other living beings is just this capacity to reason, to form abstract ideas and be guided by them. (That there may be many subconscious motivations pulling us does not mitigate this reality—the point is that even those can be properly addressed only if we think about them. Psychologists may insist that much of our lives are governed by such subconscious motives, yet they also want to bring them to our conscious awareness so we can deal with them properly.)

Even this is not enough to get to the bottom of the story, however. We must also consider the issue of causality—and what kinds of causes can exist. If the only kind of causation possible is efficient causation—the sort we illustrate with the behavior of balls being moved around on a pool table, strictly in accordance with the laws of physics—that would pretty much rule out the self-causation manifested by free will. But if a sufficiently complex entity could indeed cause events to occur without being ultimately impelled to do so by external causes, then there is room for the kind of action assumed to take place in human life that is subject to moral and political assessment.[19]

It should be noted here that several philosophers have held that a determinist—at least a soft determinist—view makes room for morality conceived as a system using encouragement and discouragement to influence human conduct. Yet even to advise that we ought to hold this soft-determinist viewpoint assumes that we are free to hold another, a concession that is incompatible with both hard and soft determinism. Indeed, if each instance of our conduct is but another billiard ball in an endless series of efficient causal relations, the only conclusion that makes sense is the one expressed in the song, "Que sera, sera; Whatever will be, will be." On this view, human conduct would differ only in complexity from the behavior of plants and the lower animals, and moral agency would be an illusion.[20]

There are serious difficulties with any such deterministic view, certainly. The first problem is that it is inconsistent with all that we can observe of human life. For example, we typically distinguish between prejudice and objective judgment in the context of scientific and judicial work, but such a distinction does not make sense if our minds are determined, even just "softly," to see things in certain ways and we have no self-control over whether and how they work. If I must see the world as a socialist or capitalist, there is nothing that I can do to accommodate that injunction that I ought to be unbiased as I assess arguments concerning public policy. If my mind is wired to see blacks as more prone to crime than whites, then if a judge implores me in my capacity as a juror to take an unbiased view of the evidence and law, this instruction is pointless. Everything we do wrong—from polluting a creek to murder—would have to be regarded as a matter of illness or abnormality, at any rate nothing blameworthy. The normal distinction between those who choose the wrong thing and those compelled to do it would vanish.

We cannot explore the problems of determinism in full here. Suffice it to note that there is another way of understanding human conduct, namely, as *caused by the individual agent*, an entity the nature of which is complex enough to include certain self-regulatory capacities. Billiard balls and human beings are simply very different kinds of entities and therefore differ dramatically in the kinds of action they are capable of. (It would be odd to claim, for example, that it is a mere illusion that birds fly on their own power simply because billiard balls cannot fly on their own power. Billiard balls lack wings; they also lack consciousness and the ability to reason.)

The ultimate refutation of determinism is our direct observation of our own capacity to choose. We consciously experience ourselves making choices, and this experience is not a dream. In drafting a theory of human nature, we must start with the evident facts, as opposed to molding facts to fit a preconceived theory. And what we can observe is that within limits, every human being not crucially incapacitated can take the initiative to act and is responsible for that action.[21]

To illuminate the self-caused nature of human agency, perhaps it would help to contrast it not only with the instinctive behavior of the lower animals but also with the seemingly more sophisticated "mental" capacities of certain very complex machines. Can machines be rational? What about Big Blue, IBM's powerful chess machine? I submit that the program as it churns away is more like the billiard ball in its predictable motions than it is like the self-regulatory action of human will.

Computers are great at rapid calculation, just as humans have designed them to be. They are faster than us when it comes to adding, subtracting, or executing a winning chess strategy. But what humans do that no computer can yet do is inaugurate a subroutine at will, on the entity's own untutored initiative. Human thinking is self-generated and self-regulatory; we can witness and inspect what is going on in our own minds and alter its course. We can turn it on or off on our own, without any instruction tapped into a keyboard. Machines, by contrast, operate *automatically*, no matter how complex their operations may be. They may, when cleverly programmed, give the appearance of intuitive, intelligent interaction with a rational interlocutor. But that simulation is itself ultimately the product of outside intervention rather than any kind of path taking that can be characterized as *chosen.*

This is why, when a machine malfunctions, it makes no sense to blame it, any more than it makes sense to blame animals for instinctively leaping on prey that happens to be you. And that is also why believers in animal rights and artificial thinking machines address their arguments not to nonhuman animals or powerful digital computers but, simply and solely, to their fellow human beings. They know that human beings alone possess the capacity to choose to think in certain ways and to stop thinking in others—to change their minds, in other words.

Now when computers and chimps begin, on their own initiative, to hold conferences about human intelligence and animal rights or trade barbs about an issue on *The McLaughlin Group,* perhaps then we can begin to seriously consider whether they have evolved into moral beings like ourselves.

ON TO ETHICS

Let us, then, take it as established beyond a reasonable doubt that humans are self-responsible and that ethics, a theory of right and wrong, is possible. Now we can talk about whether human beings have done the right thing vis-à-vis the environment. Have they disposed of their wastes responsibly? Have they cleared forests wisely? Have they built their dwellings prudently? Have they exploited resources with care and caution?

In addition to moral agency, we also need standards. There

is no point to asking whether we have done right by the environment if "right" and "wrong" aren't objectively distinguishable. If environmental activists are no more than a lobby group for state-provided outdoor health clubs or wildlife preserves, with no ability to explain why their goals have merit, the entire environmentalist movement would be a fraud. For their claims and urgings to have persuasive force, they must rest on more than merely the likes and dislikes of those who engage in politicking.

The broadest moral standards set the terms for less fundamental standards, and these broadest standards are set by the requirements of our most basic moral task, namely, to succeed as human beings—to survive and flourish. What we should do in pursuit of this end often involves the transformation and use of the natural world of which we are a part. We have the moral responsibility to engage in the needed transformation and use in a conscientious, thoughtful fashion. We can fail to do this (and we fail too often). But we can also succeed. That, too, is implicit in the field of environmental ethics.

To succeed, we must learn what nature contains with which we may achieve our highly varied tasks in life, tasks that enable us to live our lives as our nature, including our individuality, requires. For example, to discover whether a medicine can cure us of an illness and is safe to use, we might require the use of animals and plants.

Why would it be morally proper for us to make such use of nature? We know from our study of the rest of the living world that doing well at living is what it means, at least predominantly, to be good. Our evaluations in zoology, botany, biology, and medicine make this clear—the good is that which is conducive to survival, and the bad is that which is destructive of survival.[22] When we come to human life, the same general standard obtains. And for human beings to make use of other organisms for pro-life purposes follows the natural pattern. All lower animals make use of other animals or plants in order to remain alive; life feeds on life, of necessity. But for human beings, the sustenance of life now entails a moral dimension, and the sustenance of human lives includes whatever is required to give our moral nature scope, including the implementation of certain sociopolitical principles.

There are those, of course, who claim that much or all of what human beings create to improve their lives constitutes an unnatural and artificial intrusion on nature. But human beings—including all their faculties and potentials—are as much a part of nature as all the lesser-endowed animals. Their activities—from football and bowling to building tunnels, burning fossil fuels, driving cars, and holding philosophy conferences—are as natural as it is for the bee to make honey, the swallow to fly south in winter, or the beaver to dam creeks. Human life is a form of natural life. Whatever derives from its consistent development or realization is in accordance with nature; whatever subverts or corrupts it is not.[23]

What is true of human beings is that their moral faculty enables them to mismanage their lives, in effect, to subvert their own nature, by choice. But what would such subversion consist of?

It would be to conduct oneself irrationally, by evading what is most healthy and productive for one's life and therefore living a vicious rather than virtuous life. Thinking is work. It is not automatic—and, indeed, ethics itself rests on the view that human beings can choose.

Within the parameters of these broad standards, a great deal of the diverse things that human beings do can be perfectly natural, even when it is destructive of—or, to speak more precisely, transforms and utilizes—certain other aspects of nature. The rational thing for us to do is to make the best use of nature. That does not mean we should employ no guidelines in using nature. But it does mean we use nature—unabashedly and as productively as possible—to serve human goals and aspirations.

Reverence for Life, Reverence for Rights

Now we are ready to enter the realm of politics and law. The value dimension of human life has social, economic, and political implications, chief among which is the necessity of individual human rights.

Why individual *human* rights? As I discussed in chapter 1, the rights being spoken of are justified by reference to the human capacity to make moral choices. For instance, if each of us has the right to life, liberty, and property—as well as more specialized rights connected with politics, the press, and religion—we do so because we have as our central task in life to act morally in pursuit of our well-being, and this task needs to be shielded against intrusive actions from other moral agents. To engage in responsible and sound moral judgment and conduct throughout the scope of our lives, we require a reasonably clear sphere of personal jurisdiction—a domain in which we are sovereign and can either succeed or fail to live well.

If we did not have rights, we would not have such a sphere of personal jurisdiction and there could be no clear idea as to whether we are acting in our own behalf or those of other persons. A kind of *moral tragedy of the commons* would ensue, with an indeterminate measure of *moral dumping and sharing* without responsibility being assignable to anyone for either.[24] No one could be clearly blamed or praised for the various social consequences of his or her actions, for we would not know clearly

enough if what someone does is within his or her own authority. Instead of acknowledging and giving scope to our moral
nature, such a politics would flout our nature. This is the problem that arises in communal living and, especially, in totalitarian
countries, where everything is under forced collective gover-
nance. The reason moral distinctions are still possible to make
under such circumstances is that in fact—as distinct from law—
there is always some sphere of personal jurisdiction wherein
people may exhibit such virtues as courage, prudence, justice,
integrity, and honesty. But where collectivism has been most
fully enforced, there is no individual responsibility at all. It is
swallowed up by the collective.

In the past—and in many places even today—it was
thought that government rightly exercises an overwhelming
leadership role in human communities. This belief followed
from the view that human beings differ among themselves radically, some being lower-class, some higher-class, some possessing divine rights, others lacking them, some having a personal
communion with God, others lacking this special advantage.
With such views permeating a society, it made sense to argue
that government should exercise a patriarchal role. It is in op-
position to this viewpoint that John Locke argued his theory of
natural individual human rights.[25]

We have seen that the most sensible and influential doctrine of human rights rests on the fact that human beings are
indeed members of a discernibly different species. Central to
what distinguishes human beings from other animals is that
they are moral agents and thus have as their central objective in
life to live morally well, to live by principles of right and wrong
in their personal lives and in their communities. Rights enforce
and protect a social scope for the exercise of this moral agency.

This attendance to the requirements of human flourishing is what a reverence for human life must entail; not being moral agents, the lower animals cannot be a part of this circle of rights. The feature that distinguishes human beings from other living beings is that we are creative, self-conscious, thinking biological entities. To live our lives worthy of reverence, we must actualize these capacities. We ought to live productive, creative, inventive, active lives, ones that remain alert to reality and our relationship to it. We ought to live "examined lives," as Socrates advised, rather than self-deceived and lazy ones.

And we ought to see to it that this is something possible to everyone with whom we are in contact. As Aristotle noted, we are indeed political animals, closely tied to others and in need of principles to guide our relationship to them.

Given what human beings are—creative, self-conscious, thinking, choosing animals—what we need is an anthropocentric polity of liberty. This polity is not one in which we would be subservient to the will of others, even if that be the will of a majority. The laws of a just, good human community must express our reverence for our capacity for choice. As the American Declaration of Independence puts it, we have the rights, among others, to life, liberty, and the pursuit of happiness. And this is what needs to be revered most highly in our public affairs, which is why governments are instituted "to secure" these rights.

None of such public principles can even begin to be practiced by nonhuman animals. Even so, a crucial assumption of a nonanthropocentric environmental ethics is the view that at least animals and maybe even plants are as valuable as human beings, possibly even to the extent that the law should acknowledge animal rights and the legal standing of plants.

No doubt many environmental ethicists sincerely believe

they have good reason to oppose anthropocentrism. They seem to hold that anthropocentrism implies that human beings may exercise a random, capricious control over the rest of nature. Yet many environmentalists might reconsider their perspective if they became convinced that anthropocentrism does not endorse rapaciousness and is by no means in any inherent conflict with the rational management of the environment.

Not only does a perspective that favors human life above all appear to be better justified in terms of the requirements of human life itself; by encouraging self-responsibility, a human-first orientation also generates public policy that is as hospitable as possible to the world around us, given that we are indeed justified in exploiting that natural world for human ends. Let's turn to this question in the next chapter.

3

A SOUND
ENVIRONMENTALISM

I was flying from Orange County to San Jose on a clear, beautiful California day, and as the plane passed over the Channel
Island across from Santa Barbara, I realized why I do not trust
certain environmentalists.

Several years earlier, I had taken a boat out there with a
bunch of other people, and we spent the day roaming about
the island, enjoying its sights and sounds. At the time, a rancher
family owned it. Then it passed into the hands of the National
Park Service, and for a while all visits to the islands were
banned. Now it appears that visits are allowed once again. But
no building by private parties is permitted there, certainly
nothing that would make it possible for ordinary folks to spend
a few days relaxing on the islands without bringing "all your
own food, water, and camping equipment," as the National
Park Service website stipulates. "Roughing it" is, apparently,
the only kind of interaction with this environment that is officially sanctioned.

As I flew over the islands, I thought about how much I'd
enjoy it if there were a commercial establishment there that

could enable folks like me to stay a day or so and enjoy the beautiful environment. Yes, I sure would like it. What I didn't think was that I am *entitled* to it, that I have a right to go to those islands on the terms most favorable to me. I merely figured that if a private party could own the place, he could decide to make room for me in exchange for a few coins; and he would, indeed, have every incentive to do so.

But instead, certain folks got some laws passed making it a criminal act for someone to purchase land on the island and build there—imposing their will by force at the expense of the wishes and hopes of the rest of us.

A sound environmentalism—one that puts humans first—would not countenance coercively enforced privilege for a particular clique of humans. Instead, it would acknowledge the essentially individual, self-responsible nature, and equal rights of all human beings. It would recognize that each member of a human community is sovereign and that no one may exercise rule over another without that other's consent. In practice, public policy based on such principles would allow land to be bought and sold freely, without anyone being authorized to wield the power of use and disposal over land that they have merely appropriated rather than obtained fair and square in the marketplace. It would be an environmentalism based on the principles of justice, property rights, due process, and freedom.

NATURE, RIGHTS, AND SOCIETY

The individual rights approach to human community life is the only one that most readily accommodates human nature and beneficial human interaction with the natural ecology of which human beings are a part. To be sure, human action has some-times been inconsistent with both ecological well-being and human well-being. But how do we know what kinds of human action might have been more or less conducive to flourishing? Only by consulting the facts of human nature and what these imply for their conduct within the natural world. If human be-ings have basic rights to life, liberty, and property, then such rights are perfectly consistent with our place in the natural world; they in fact manifest our nature.

Of course, the natural environment is altered by the pres-ence of human beings just as nature is altered by the presence of any species. Human beings have a greater power than other species to alter nature, and we may do so reasonably or not. But the mere fact of our exploitation of nature and other animals is no more "intrusive" or improper, per se, than that of any other species doing what it takes to survive.

Efforts to keep the Channel Islands of the world out of pri-vate hands are just one symptom of a larger ethical–political in-terventionist public policy, the one that is justified by the alleged antithesis between individual good and "common good." If environmentalists claim that the power conferred on individuals by the right to private property is hazardous to the common welfare,[1] so do some criminologists when they claim that upholding the individual rights of the accused threatens the good of the community by helping some criminals go unpun-ished, and so do our arbiters of personal morality when they claim that upholding the individual's right to use harmful drugs undermines public morals or that freedom of commerce un-leashes the forces of greed at the expense of decency and har-mony. The curtailment of *individual* rights rarely occurs without an accompanying assertion of *public* benefit.

But does it have to be thus? Must individual rights conflict with the common welfare? Certainly those who proposed the doctrine of individual natural rights did not suppose so. It was precisely in recognition of the congruence of the protection of individuals and the health of the community that many advocated the protection of individual rights to begin with. John Locke would never have admitted the alleged conflict here. Rather, the conflict, if there is any, stems from a basic misunderstanding: the notion that the community is anything but a community *of human individuals* who share certain social concerns that will best be served if each individual has his or her rights fully protected.

Rights incorporate a fundamental recognition of the human nature that all members of society share. This recognition supplies us with standards by which community life may be fully harmonized, at least potentially. The natural rights tradition holds that such harmony is best secured by granting every individual a sphere of *personal jurisdiction*. Within this jurisdiction each person is empowered—and, yes, not being coerced by others is indeed empowerment for nearly all of us—to accomplish individual goals to the best possible extent. Properly protected personal jurisdictions limit the potential for social mischief. For by prohibiting persons from intruding on others or violating the rights of others, what the evil persons do is more likely to hurt only themselves (and voluntary associates like business partners and spouses). A polity of well-enforced rights thus systematically discourages wrongdoing—including gratuitous despoliation or damage of the environment—which, in turn, confers overall benefit to the community.

Even many thinkers who believed that the best course of conduct for everyone is to serve the community believed, along with Bernard Mandeville and Adam Smith, that public benefit could be procured via private "vice," provided that certain principles of liberty were upheld. Even earlier, Aristotle suggested that the right to private property would enhance public welfare.[2]

One way to support the idea of the harmony of individual rights and the common good is to demonstrate the compossibility of individual goods and rights—meaning that no one's objective, fundamental good need obstruct another's objective good, in turn suggesting that the pursuit of individual goods within the framework of individual rights can bring about the maximum well-being of the community.

But are the objective goods or values of individuals really compossible, that is, fully capable of being realized for all? We are not speaking here of rights claims of the sort discussed in the first chapter of this workbook—that is, claims that are so specific in nature, such as a claim to the same piece of land, that the claims are clearly not compossible. All that is being contended here is that the exercise of very fundamental rights—which would entail a just adjudication of disputes—is possible and that my exercise of freedom and your exercise of freedom do not inherently clash, even if we might have a disagreement one day that requires arbitration.

Some argue that mutually compatible rights aren't even conceivable, let alone possible. They believe that no common human nature exists that would enable us to identify common standards of good or value. Or they argue that human nature is a myth, so that any idea of compatible values must be hopelessly futile. The facts that justify belief in a distinctively human nature were considered in the preceding chapter.

Then there are the more empirically minded critics who cite a human history replete with conflict and conclude that any belief in some kind of harmony must therefore be utopian, even if not unthinkable theoretically. But this kind of objection presupposes that the record of how people have in fact behaved is the record of how they *had* to behave. Even if we agree that historical circumstances shape the kind of alternatives that people confront, the fact that individuals are capable of *choosing among* those given alternatives is inferred from human nature itself, which persists through the ages.

Of course, it may not be possible to know exactly what might have happened instead of what in fact did happen had different principles of human conduct been more dominant in various ages. But just as it is possible to know that freeing those held in slavery would have been better all around than keeping them enslaved or that not perpetrating the Holocaust would have been better than perpetrating it, so, too, it is possible to know that certain political–social policies are superior to others even when the alternatives are not so stark.

As far as our environmental woes are concerned, consistent, wide-ranging implementation of the right to private property would have worked out best. Societies with the highest degree of voluntariness in human relations are arguably the best ones. When people have their right to choose respected and protected—to their right, for example, to seek and to dispose of their assets and with whom to associate—they are likely to be more careful and attentive to what they are doing. And so the best approach to environmental issues is to privatize. That is how responsible environmental management is best encouraged (though never guaranteed, as it certainly isn't when government takes on the task, either).

Moreover, the idea of a common good that exists somehow over and above individual goods is itself problematic. How are we to identify a transcendent specific common good in the first place—that is, a "good" in the sense of a common goal or end as opposed to common principles of social conduct?[3] Will any candidate for such a "common good" not always be the candidate of some special group of human beings and thus by definition not the *common* good? Is there even such a being as humanity or society apart from the individuals who comprise it, with all their individual and varying values and goals? What else can there be but the good of individuals?

Yet when it comes to environmental matters, few who call themselves environmentalists believe that there is no inherent conflict between the individual good and the common welfare. Consider the alleged problem of the ozone layer. It seems that in the long run the right of individuals to secure for themselves, for example, refrigeration and air conditioning simply cannot help but clash with the prospects for a healthy human race. Free trade, the freedom to pursue happiness, even the freedom to express oneself seem to some not to be rights but rather occasional, highly circumscribed privileges that can and should be revoked whenever the environment or some other value deemed to be "higher" is purportedly being threatened by them.

In fact, environmental well-being and other human social values are not only compatible with but also dependent on respect for individual rights. Although it seems counterintuitive to some environmentalists, it should not come as a surprise that the environment is better managed when the realities of human nature are recognized rather than ignored, just as human society is "better managed" when individuals are allowed to choose their own paths, as long as they do not interfere with the rights of others to do the same.

It is no coincidence that totalitarian societies like those of the Soviet Union or Saddam-era Iraq have been the ones that suffer the highest levels of both social and environmental destruction. But although economic central planning has become somewhat discredited, the desire to "preserve" the environment remains a popular rationale for coercive, centralized government control over our lives—and for bans on private ownership and control.

ECOLOGY: A NEW
EXCUSE FOR STATISM?

In recent decades, collectivist political economies have fallen into some disrepute. There were theoretical hints of why collectivist planning is doomed to failure as far back as the fourth century B.C., when, in the *Politics*, Aristotle observed that private ownership of property encourages responsible human behavior more readily than does the collectivism spelled out in Plato's *Republic*.

In our own time, the same general observation was advanced in more technical and rigorous terms by Ludwig von Mises in his 1922 (German edition) book *Socialism*,[4] although he was concerned mainly with more general economic problems of production and allocation of resources for satisfying individual preferences. More recently, Garrett Hardin has argued[5] that the difficulties first observed by Aristotle plague us in the context of the quintessentially public realm: the ecological environment.

But such indictments of collectivism, coupled with the few moral arguments against it, failed to dissuade many intellectuals from attempting to implement it. The past century was filled with enthusiastic, stubborn, visionary, opportunistic, and bloody efforts to enact the collectivist dream. Not until the collapse of the Soviet attempt, in the form of its Marxist–Leninist internationalist socialist revolution, did it dawn on most people that collectivism was simply not going to enable people to live a decent life. Although most admit that in small units—convents, kibbutzes, the family—a limited, temporary collectivist arrangement may be feasible, they are no longer hopeful about transforming entire societies into centrally planned tribes.

A recent admission of the failure of economic collectivism in the wake of the collapse of the Soviet bloc economy comes from Professor Robert Heilbroner, one of socialism's most intelligent and loyal champions for the past several decades. "Ludwig von Mises . . . had written of the 'impossibility' of socialism, arguing that no Central Planning Board could ever gather the enormous amount of information needed to create a workable economic system. . . . It turns out, of course, that Mises was right."[6]

But, like other thinkers who have seen their utopian schemes implode, Heilbroner cannot quite say good-bye to all that. He believes that there are two ways the collectivist dream might be salvaged. First, it may leave us with at least piecemeal social objectives to strive for, even if any advances toward them must always occur in the context of essentially capitalist economic systems. Second, collectivist policy could reemerge in a more viable form as an instrument of the ecological movement.

> [If] there is any single problem that will have to be faced by any socioeconomic order over the coming decades it is the problem of making our economic peace with the demands of the environment. Making that peace means insuring that the vital processes of material provisioning do not contaminate the green-blue film on which life itself depends. This imperative need not affect all social formations, but none so profoundly as capitalism.[7]

What is one to say about this new problem, a problem allegedly too complicated for free men and women to handle?

Has Heilbroner never heard of the "tragedy of the commons"? Can he not imagine the environmental difficulties that face the collectivist social systems?

> It is, perhaps, possible that some of the institutions of capitalism—markets, dual realms of power, even private ownership of some kind of production—may be adapted to that new state of ecological vigilance, but, if so, they must be monitored, regulated, and contained to such a degree that it would be difficult to call the final social order capitalism.[8]

This superficially novel but essentially old-fashioned skepticism about free-market capitalism needs to be addressed.

My first response is that there is no justification for greater distrust of "the market" than of the scientific bureaucracy that would be charged with doing the monitoring, regulating, and containing that Heilbroner and so many other champions of regimentation plump for. Such sweeping distrust of voluntary processes tends to arise from comparing the market system to some ideal and static construct developed in the mind of a theorist—not to real alternatives.

Since human community life is dynamic, the best way to improve it is by the establishment of certain basic principles of law, or a constitution, that will keep the dynamics of the community within certain bounds.[9] But if human agents in the marketplace, guided by the rule of law based on their natural individual rights to life, liberty, and property, are by nature incapable of meeting the ecological challenges Heilbroner and many others in the environmentalist movement have in mind, one wonders how these challenges could be better met by some "new" brand of statism.

After all, why should we expect ecologically minded bureaucrats to be somehow better motivated, more competent, and more virtuous than all those socialist bureaucrats who expressed so much concern for the poor and the hungry and the unjustly treated workers of the world? Why attribute to an ecological politburo any greater wisdom and nobility than has ever been manifested by a socialist politburo? If free men and women will not manage the environment capably, neither will anyone else.

Let us for the sake of argument understand Heilbroner not to be advocating full-fledged collectivism but rather a compromise between an individualist–capitalist system and a collectivist system—that is, the welfare state. After all, he stipulates that the ecologically prudent socioeconomic system he envisions would be substantially individualist insofar as the institution of private property would not be entirely abolished in such a system. On the other hand, it is a system that would be "monitored, regulated, and contained to such a degree that it would be difficult to call the final social order capitalism."

That sound you hear is a sigh of exasperation. Do we really need once again to abandon the individualist alternative for some increasingly regimented social order?

Let us consider why an individual rights approach will more likely resolve environmental problems and, thus, be more conducive to the common good—as understood within a framework that acknowledges the ontological priority of human individuals over their various groupings—than alternatives that propose to chronically violate individual rights. While this may seem question begging—by denying at the outset any meaningful non-individualist sense of the common good—it will turn out not to be once the individualist environmentalism that emerges comes to full light. (Indeed, how could a systemic intervention be for the common good if various members of the community are habitually harmed by it?)

An Unpolluted Concept of Rights

First, we need to stress what the individual rights position on pollution actually is. Whenever pollution-generating activities cannot be carried out without clear injury to nonconsenting third parties, such activities must be prohibited as inherently violating the rights of others. The injury must be demonstrable, not merely hypothetical. This requirement would not permit a ban on trade in pesticide-treated fruits, for example, given the fact that the risk of eating such fruit is lower than or equal to normal risks encountered in everyday life.

Under property rights, emissions that might eventually add up to actionable pollution are allowable only when they occur below a certain threshold. When the threshold is passed, then and only then can the emission be construed as actually polluting (that is, actually harmful to persons) rather than simply defiling. In some contexts, a system of first-come, first-served might be instituted, so that those who start the production first would be permitted to continue, while others, who would raise the threshold to a harmful level, would not. This may appear arbitrary, but in fact numerous areas of human life, including especially commerce, make use of such a criterion, and human ingenuity could well be expended to make sure that one's firm is not a latecomer.

The earth—as well as any part of the universe where life support is reasonably imaginable—can often absorb some measure of potentially injurious waste. (After all, life itself produces waste!) Most toxic substances can dissipate up to a point. Barring the privatization of such spheres in such a way that they can be kept apart and separated from others, a judicially efficient management of toxic substance disposal must take into consideration how far disposal can continue before the vital point—up until which the waste can be harmlessly absorbed and dissipated—is reached. Technical measurements would need to be correlated with information about the levels of human tolerance for the toxic substance in question. Risk analysis would need to be performed so as to learn whether the risk of falling victim to toxic substance disposal corresponds with or exceeds the typical risks of everyday life not associated with pollution.

It is important to note that a natural rights, individualist standard of tolerance might very well be far lower than even those who support it would imagine. Many free-market advocates favor a social cost–benefit approach here based on the utilitarian idea that what ultimately matters is the achievement of some state of collective satisfaction. But this is not the approach that flows from the idea that individuals have natural negative rights to life, liberty, and property.

Assuming the soundness of the natural rights stance, it may be necessary to prepare for some drastic lifestyle changes, so that some past abuses can be rectified. For example, whereas automobile wastes have been poured into the atmosphere with an understanding that from a utilitarian perspective it is worth doing so (based on social cost–benefit analysis), from the natural rights viewpoint it might be necessary (if the harmful effects to nonconsenting third parties can be demonstrated) to insist on the full initial cost being borne by automobile drivers or owners, thereby at least temporarily prompting a considerable rise in the prices of vehicles. (That the overall cost may be born more widely since more expensive manufacturing and transportation processes would result in more expensive goods and services is not relevant here. The issue is what persons may choose to do in light of demonstrable, rights-violating harm to others.)

Certainly the government of an individualist political economy would not have the authority to rely on the utilitarian notion that those harmed by pollution must simply accept it, given the fact that the benefits of industrial growth outweigh such costs in health and property damage as are caused by pollution. Instead, the principle of strict liability would apply: The polluter or those bound by contract with the polluter would be held liable. Benefits not solicited cannot be used to rationalize rights violation if one respects the individual's right to choose, as the individualist system is committed to do.

No Prior Restraint

On the other hand, though, neither would a rights-respecting government possess the authority to exercise so-called *precautionary* measures, such as "preventive justice" or prior restraint—as many environmentalists want to do today with respect to, say, the nebulously defined threat of global warming. (Climatologists do not even agree that average global temperature will escalate dangerously over the next decades, let alone that human industrialization is the primary progenitor of global temperature change.)

The ban on prior restraint is a principle of justice according to which no one may be restrained by others in his or her conduct unless the person is thereby demonstrably violating someone's rights. While the ban has been invoked mainly to protect journalism from government interference, it also plays a role in our criminal law. For example, the Fourth Amendment to the U.S. Constitution bans unreasonable searches, and there are demands for clear and present danger and probable cause throughout the legal system so as to prevent government from acting capriciously against the people.

But our system is not consistent. Government regulations habitually fly in the face of this sound principle of justice. These regulations preempt any necessity of proof of criminal wrong-doing and assume, instead, that it is appropriate for governments to act preventively. This assumption underlies the precautionary principle so frequently resorted to by environmentalists who see apocalypse at every turn.

Europe, for example, is now buzzing with talk of governments—including the supergovernment of the European Union headquartered in Brussels—forcing measures on people in the spirit of precaution. No need to demonstrate that anyone is doing something harmful or wrong before his or her conduct may be banned or constrained. Just harboring a suspicion that something will perhaps be harmful in the future, never mind any proof to that effect, is sufficient to justify measures that violate the right to individual liberty, including, of course, various activities of business.

Once, after a public debate in which I and sundry environmentalists participated, an audience member asked a familiar but troubling question: "If some industrial process were to have a devastating environmental impact only forty years after it has occurred, would it not be important to restrict it?" The answer is that it would be mandatory *not* to restrict it—not on the basis of merely hypothetical harm. If due process of law is to be maintained as a principle of public policy, there would be no way to deal with it without any evidence of what would happen.

The fact is that while it is easy to hypothesize such a case, with nothing more than a hypothesis one can't know whether the concern is valid until the predicted negative consequences actually occur or can be reliably predicted. If such consequences do begin to occur (and can be linked with the claimed cause), the evidence should persuade the relevant judge to issue an injunction against the process. But if, as the hypothesis explicitly states, there is no evidence whatever, to act on the mere possibility can only be arbitrary. After all, hypothesizing is an easy game, and many more hypotheses go by the wayside than are eventually "proven out." A good scientist comes up with a dozen different hypotheses to explain the same fact before breakfast.

Look at it from another angle. Knowing what I know of human nature, I hypothesize that many particular people *might* act in ways to violate rights. And I can even provide evidence that members of some groups are more likely to commit crimes than others. Indeed, some police officers try to anticipate such action via what is called profiling, based on race, ethnicity, dress, demeanor, and so forth. The problem is that none of these "profile matches" constitute evidence of intent by any *particular individual* to embark on criminal conduct. And so, when used, profiling leads to injustice—false arrests, harassment, and the like.

There is, of course, a political outlook under which no problem exists with profiling and acting to prevent possible wrongdoing even in the absence of evidence. This outlook is premised on the assumption that human beings have no rights. In the absence of any concern with violating individual rights, individuals could be used and abused willy-nilly to try to divine and prevent possible problems. Preventive measures such as shutting down factories or farms could be taken without any evidence of actual or imminent rights violation simply by reference to the bare possibility that such violation could occur. Such a principle serves as a carte blanche to the thus-empowered bureaucrat, of course; not needing any evidence of wrongdoing, he can trample anyone's peaceful activities at will.

This is just what some communitarians have urged on us

with respect to other sorts of possibly harmful conduct, such as for drug abuse. Random searches of cars and even homes have been proposed as a way to stem drug-related crime. If the individuals who would be detained, searched, and tested have no rights to liberty and privacy, then, of course, subjecting them to preventive harassment would be unobjectionable—except perhaps on the grounds that it does no good and costs too much.

Many environmentalists do deny that human beings have rights—or at any rate rights of the sort that can trump concerns about the spotted owl or rare toads. But human individuals do have rights, and to restrain another person out of precaution is a license to tyranny. We all have the capacity to do wrong (as presupposed, for instance, by some of the more ludicrous excesses of post-9/11 airport security). And some of us fit certain profiles that have in the past been evident in people who have actually done something wrong. In our concern for "the environment," we must not neglect to care for our political environment. We can't allow liberty itself to become an endangered species.

If we value our liberty, we have to live with the fact that innocent people may not be imposed on even if we suspect that extensive impositions might well prevent some future disaster. We must abide by the principle of due process and reject prior restraint. (This indeed is the way to distinguish between the conduct of civilized people and criminals or, especially, terrorists, something terrorists are well aware of and exploit.[10])

THE TRAGEDY OF THE COMMONS

Whatever they may concede about the virtues of the market, Heilbroner and the rest nonetheless fail to consistently recognize that individual property owners have a direct and immediate interest in the fate of their own property—a self-interested motivation that leads them to maintain and sustain that property.

Environmentalists often dislike the very idea of what they regard as environmental treasures being controlled by private hands. After all, the right of ownership means that the owner of a particular chunk of environment is free to alter it in ways that the environmentalist might not like.

But, in the first place, there is nothing privileged about the environmentalist's values and preferences with respect to the environment as opposed to the values and preferences of those who would drill for oil or build a shopping mall or buy the oil or shop at the mall. And there is also no reason why environmentalists can't procure parts of the environment on a free market much as any business group could do. After all, as private property owners of treasured lands or waters, environmentalists are free to run their own property according to their own principles of environmental preservation without fear of bureaucratic bungling or pressure-group politics.

We talk too much about "our" water, land, mountains, or animals—for it is precisely when an environmental area is held "in common" that no one but a select group of power holders (and those who successfully lobby them) can exercise any power at all over that area. "Common" ownership is no ownership at all. You cannot give any of the "commonly held" land to your friends or children. Nor can you sell it to fund some medical treatment you may need or education you may wish to provide to your children. Nor can you even simply traverse the lands and waters and mountains, either, let alone hobnob with the animals at your heart's content.

Common ownership, so called, generates overuse and

confusion—the famous "tragedy of the commons." In practice, the destructive incentives inherent in a commons are combated by turning control over to a few. In democratic societies, this few gains control by persuading the majority of voters to give them power to put the commons to use as they see fit. In dictatorships, not even that kind of support is needed, although in both systems the power tends to fluctuate with the winds of opinion—either among the many or among the elite.

The Tragedy of the "Common Interest"

In the fourth century B.C., Aristotle identified a central principle of community life by demonstrating the social value of the right to private property:

> That all persons call the same thing mine in the sense in which each does so may be a fine thing, but it is impracticable; or if the words are taken in the other sense, such a unity in no way conduces to harmony. And there is another objection to the proposal. For that which is common to the greatest number has the least care bestowed upon it. Every one thinks chiefly of his own, hardly at all of the common interest; and only when he is himself concerned as an individual. For besides other considerations, everybody is more inclined to neglect the duty which he expects another to fulfill; as in families many attendants are often less useful than a few. (*Politics*, 1262a30 37)

This same idea was more recently clarified by Garrett Hardin in his famous 1968 article "The Tragedy of the Commons." He explained it this way:

> Picture a pasture open to all. It is to be expected that each herdsman will try to keep as many cattle as possible on the

commons. Such an arrangement may work reasonably satis-
factorily for centuries because tribal wars, poaching, and disease keep the numbers of both man and beast well bellow
the carrying capacity of the land. Finally, however, comes
the day of reckoning, that is, the day when the long desired
goal of social stability becomes a reality. At this point, the
inherent logic of the commons remorselessly generates tragedy. . . . Freedom in a commons brings ruin to all.[11]

In short, the common grazing area is used by all herdsmen to
feed their livestock. But because there are no borders identify-
ing what area belongs to whom, the commons will eventually
be overused. Each owner wants to feed his livestock as well as
possible, but any desire he might have to regulate his usage to
preserve the commons is mediated by his knowledge that he
has no way to enforce similar conduct from other herdsman.

The rational conclusion has been drawn by many scholars
that without extensive privatization of areas that are now
treated as public properties—lakes, rivers, beaches, forests, and
even the air mass—environmental problems will remain vexing
and serious.

The market is, after all, merely the result of the implementation of the principle of private property rights—the recognition that each person must have a sphere of individual
jurisdiction within which to effectuate his or her plans and purposes. Such an arrangement of a community, into individual
realms of authority, tends in the main to facilitate responsible
conduct. There can, of course, be exceptions—we can't prevent irrationality altogether, even by establishing the most natural and useful organizational social principles. Even at great
cost to themselves, people will sometimes misbehave.

Yet it makes sense that when this cost does not affect individual agents or affects them so remotely that the connection

between their actions and the consequences that follow is very difficult to observe, confusion and mismanagement are more likely. And what is a human-created ecological crisis but the macroresult of such individual confusion and mismanagement—individual persons dumping their potentially harmful waste onto the lives of others without having to incur a direct cost to themselves?

Clearly, the ecological realms most adversely affected by human agency are public realms—the air mass, lakes, oceans, many parks and beaches, and, for that matter, the treasuries of democratic states (for what is deficit spending but a tragedy of the commons?). The ultimate harm, of course, befalls individual human beings—now or in the future—and other living things on which human life often depends or from which it gains a great deal of benefit and satisfaction. Yet the harms occur in ways that are not judicially manageable, for the links between culprits and victims are neither detectable nor actionable.

As already noted, integral to a normative environmentalism is the idea of individual moral responsibility. To even implore others to do the right thing assumes they have a choice to make. To criticize them assumes they could have done otherwise and should, on their own initiative, have done the right thing. But if human beings do not have a realm of personal authority, a sphere of jurisdiction within which their judgments guide their conduct, the preconditions for responsible action are missing or undermined. Acting in a commons, individuals can submerge their obligations within the undifferentiated actions of the group. And no one need face, let alone admit, moral guilt for wrongdoing.

Most people have a clear enough idea that so-called common ownership causes problems. Such ordinary phenomena as littering, and the neglect of public parks and beaches is evident to us, even if we do not then apply the manifest principle to other vital areas of social life. But nothing much can be done about the problem where it exists without a systematic conversion of the commons to private property.

Inertia is one stumbling block. But it is also just very difficult in some cases to subject certain valued resources to privatization—for example, air and water. Accordingly, even among those who are fully persuaded of the need for privatization, the political will and savvy to achieve the solution lags far behind the analysis that identified the solution. Indeed, Hardin himself was reluctant to embrace libertarian solutions and hoped, instead, that government policies would somehow be enlisted to dampen the tragedy, kind of like adding tape to a Band-Aid that is too small for the wound.

Even when we do begin to introduce market solutions, the potential benefits may be hard to discern given the continuing presence of the commons and the attendant distorting incentives. Consider toll roads, which are more expensive to drive than "freeways" but which I find so much less aggravating to drive than freeways and other public roads. And I probably get my investment back anyway. My guess is that if I pay one dollar to drive the toll road, I get back nearly all that, considering the time and gas costs saved when I don't have to stop and start repeatedly (as I do on a non–toll road).

There has been a lot of gleeful toll-road bashing in the local media where I live. Writers are delighted that toll roads have not reaped all the projected benefits. And I am sure that some wishful thinking went into conceiving them.

But suppose there were a new weekly newspaper of high quality, containing all kinds of information and reasonably entertaining articles, selling for about two dollars but competing with a subsidized weekly publication of comparable content that is being given away free—the latter of which is popular in large part precisely because it is free, even though the articles aren't quite as good as those of its new competitor. Would one expect the two-dollar publication to take off and do very well in that kind of commercial climate?

No. Not instantly, anyway. People would continue plucking up the free rag, while the new publication would have an uphill battle on its hands—a battle it might win, but with greater difficulty than if its competitor had been charging, too. Something like that happens with the toll roads and would happen during other transitions to private ownership. Massive public subsidies confer an unfair advantage over firms struggling to compete as if there were a fully free market.

Aside from the patience to see transitions through, the main thing we need to solve the tragedy of the commons is a theory of justice that is fully informed by Aristotle and Hardin's recognition of the problem. Libertarianism is the only such theory afoot, and the somewhat sequestered status of libertarianism among political theories doesn't bode well for the prospects for such developments, at least not in the short run. Of course, the long run counts, too.

The Treasury as a Commons

Thinkers of all stripes tend to understand the problem with unlimited usage of land or water held "in common." What has not been as widely understood is that a tragedy of the commons exists as well in our national treasury. Recognizing the applicability of the analysis to public finance will help us understand the universal applicability of some features of economic analysis. That might incline us to look on the tragedy of the commons as more significant than has been hitherto thought for purposes of gleaning some insights about the nature of justice itself. If, furthermore, we consider the significance of the principle that "ought implies can" for a theory of justice, it could turn out that some extant theories, such as egalitarianism, will have to be seriously rethought and ultimately shelved.

In the public treasury, we have what by law amounts to a common pool of resources from which members of the political community may try to extract as much as will serve their purposes, with little thought to the aggregate negative economic consequences. These include red ink, high taxes, or loss of productivity nationwide—consequences that any particular group's pelf grabbing can only minutely affect. Whether for artistic, educational, scientific, agricultural, athletic, medical, or general moral and social progress, the treasury is regarded as a common pool that all citizens in a democratic society may dip into.

And, of course, nearly everyone has very sound reasons for dipping into it—their goals are usually well enough thought out that they have confidence in their plans. They know that if they receive support from the treasury, they can further these goals. So they graze this commons as much as their political power will enable them to.

Any commons is going to be exploited by individual agents without regard to standards or limits—which explains, at least in part, why the treasuries of most Western democracies are being slowly depleted, deficits are growing without any sign of restraint, and such political limits as do persist tend to gradually wither away. Japan, Germany, Great Britain, and, of course, the United States are all experiencing this common looting of the treasury, as are numerous other societies that make public funds available for private purposes. For how else can we construe education, scientific research, the building of athletic parks, the upkeep of beaches, forests, and so forth except as the funding of special private goals by means of a common treasury?

Some might try to obscure this fact by claiming that all these goals do involve a public dimension. Of course. But so does nearly every private purpose. Private goals can have public benefits. But qua *private* goals, their main function is to serve the specific interests of specific individuals. In the commons, individuals enjoy the benefits of pursuing their interests at the public trough without having to contend directly with the costs of doing so. When AIDS research is supported publicly, the first beneficiaries of success are those with AIDS, not those who haven't yet contracted the disease. When theater groups gain support from the National Endowment for the Arts, there may be beneficiaries beyond those obtaining funding, but the theater groups benefit directly and immediately. When milk producers gain a federal subsidy by having the price of milk fixed or their withholding of production compensated, they are the ones who gain from this, not some wider public (and the public in fact loses doubly—by having to subsidize nonproduction and by having to pay higher prices for milk). Such is the case with thousands of other "public" projects—first and foremost, they promote private and individual goals—the goals of particular, individual, specific human begins.

And there is no end in sight. Only when the country no longer enjoys creditworthiness in the eyes of the world community, so that hopeful lenders will no longer buy its bonds, will the Ponzi scheme be called to a halt. The government will then have to declare bankruptcy.

Road to Solutions

There is no quick and easy way to escape the tragedy of the commons. To many people, privatization and laissez-faire are jarring proposals. Yet without such radical solutions, the problem is intractable. Any effort to handle it by way of democratic or republican public policy can only dampen or defer the problem. Soon the tragedy must reemerge, as lobbyists and special-interest groups accommodate themselves to new political circumstances.

Governments use force to accomplish their goals. But force, unless used in self-defense—as the military is supposed to use it—wreaks havoc in its path, even when the ostensible results seem to be grand.[12] And nowhere is this more evident than in environmental matters. When the laws and public policy favor the system of eminent domain and the use of publicly owned lands and waters for whatever happens to be in quasi-democratic demand, the usual result is akin to a zero-sum game: The favored policy wins, the disfavored one loses. By contrast, in the free market, there are many disparate demands that get satisfied to a greater or lesser extent. This has vital implications for environmental policy.

In the case of public finance, only if the treasury stops allowing private projects to be funded at all from its coffers—confining itself to the support of bona fide public projects like the courts, the military, and police—will there be an end that avoids the perhaps greatest tragedy of the commons. To reach such a position of financial responsibility, governments will have to sell off all the unwisely held common assets—lands, parks, beaches, buildings, forests, lakes, and such—to private parties. They will thus liberate members of our future generations from the ever welling costs that have been so irresponsibly imposed on them by means of the proliferation of the commons.

This by itself does not solve all problems that face us in the wake of the tragedy of the commons. The air and water masses of the globe can't be privatized, at least not for the time being. The way to discourage their abuse will have to be researched; it may be found in the law of personal injury and trespass. People who traverse the public realm will have to confine their conduct to that which is peaceful and noninjurious, lest they find themselves charged with criminal assault and trespass. In any case, acknowledgment of the tragedy of the commons must precede any serious research program that needs to be mounted in order to inch closer to solutions.

THE MERITS OF THE CLASSICAL LIBERAL INFRASTRUCTURE

Societies in which private property makes it possible for one to enjoy a significant measure of sovereignty are certainly better off than those growing in levels of involuntary servitude—even with respect to the highest or noblest goals one can imagine, including environmental rectitude.[13] This is beyond any reasonable doubt. Alas, unreasonable doubt does tend to dominate politics, so millions still denounce substantially free societies—as witness the raging objections to the ideals of the North American Free Trade Agreement and the World Trade Organization. (Not that the policies of these organizations are never objectionable; my point is only that their main goals, the removal of trade barriers throughout global commerce, are commendable.) Most environmentalists propose political solutions to problems they see with the environment and support state regimentation as the default solution to whatever problem they perceive. Michael Kelly, the *Atlantic Monthly* editor who died in a tragic accident during Operation Iraqi Freedom and who was a very fine writer and thinker on many fronts, offered a line of criticism of the radical libertarian, free-market thesis in the *Atlantic*'s June/May 2001 issue. Kelly argues that, if you think that it is private individuals working in voluntary cooperation who make good things happen, think again:

> If we look at the great moments in innovation, the developments that changed everything, we almost always find that the private geniuses did their bit, but the great clumsy, heavy hand of government is frequently what turned that bit into a new way of life. Ford gave us the cheap car, but Eisenhower gave us the interstate. Edison gave us the light bulb, but the TVA wired the farms. Most of the great advances in flight, and all the advances in space flight, have their origins in government—specifically military—work. So, too, with the Internet, which rose out of the government's ARPANET system. It was government that linked America's coasts by rail, government that constructed the Panama Canal, government that built all the really big stuff. The revolution in flight . . . came about not only because of the work of private geniuses but also because a bunch of bureaucrats at NASA pushed it, and because those bureaucrats were lucky to have had as their boss since 1992 an engineer named Daniel Goldin.

Anyone familiar with the history of political economic thought will have serious doubts about Kelly's remarks. There is, for starters, Frederick Bastiat's argument, presented in his essay "That Which Is Seen, and That Which Is Not Seen,"[14] in which it is shown that although what governments do often takes center stage on the historical and reportorial scene, it is folly to forget that the resources invested in such doings are invested at the expense of a lot else that might have happened had government not substituted its one-size-fits-all judgment for that of voluntarily cooperating individuals.

Let us look at some of what Kelly lists as creditable to government and whether credit really is all that warranted. Take Eisenhower and the interstate highway system. No one can reasonably dispute that this federal policy gave a very serious boost to the automobile and in the process suppressed, most likely, the development of alternative, probably more environmentally friendly modes of transportation.

Or take the Tennessee Valley Authority (TVA), which has pretty much been discredited as the great boon to farmers its champions painted.[15] The TVA was by no means a godsend to all, as some have maintained. Most of those in the region had electricity already, with TVA simply grabbing up many of the existing power companies. As a result of the TVA's work, all the best farmland in the Tennessee Valley was placed underwater. Farmers were kicked off their lands, forced to sell at below market prices. Many died prematurely as a result of the stress.

The Tellico Dam fiasco became famous because of the snail darter, but it was a botched project even without the ex post facto intervention of the flawed Endangered Species Act (which implied that saving the snail darter was far more important than salvaging the millions of dollars and years of human effort that had gone into the dam). Before the act ever came along, landowners had been kicked off their lands even though they were in no danger of being submerged by water. The TVA sold their land to developers and figured in the potential profits as part of their cost–benefit analysis. Of course, TVA's environmental impact is now considered to be devastating.

The ARPANET system did give rise to the Internet, but,

as many historians argue, that inaugural act was of minimal significance.[16] The initial ARPANET was clumsy, and only after a demand for the service developed did it become efficient and useful. Kelly is right—as is former Vice President Al Gore—that the initial ideas that produced the Internet came from efforts by the Department of Defense to enhance the defense of the country. However, these ideas could have developed independently, and once a market for them emerged having nothing to do with state matters, the technology became more productive than before—America Online, Yahoo, Prodigy, Juno, Netscape, Internet Explorer, and all the rest working feverishly to create ever evolving solutions to the communication and information needs of fickle consumers.

As to the railways that government has subsidized, one result was massive monopolies that later were used to justify antitrust legislation and that have run roughshod over private farming across the country. In the case of the Transcontinental Railroad, it was a subsidized fiasco. One of the consequences of this monstrosity was the early attempt to wipe out the Native Americans. The railroad certainly hastened their demise, especially since it came so soon after the Civil War when folks like Sherman and Sheridan were still in command and eager to eliminate the Native Americans altogether.[17]

The history of the railroad industry is mixed; not all railroads were heavily entangled with government. But if the government had kept out of the picture altogether, economic motives to expand travel routes would still have existed. The premier contemporary example of government-subsidized passenger rail is, of course, Amtrak—a chronic fiscal basket case whose current president, David Gunn, suggests that it is "fanciful" to expect that Amtrak could ever be self-supporting.[18]

Another boondoggle writ large was the Panama Canal.

First the French government tried to dig it through some of the most impenetrable regions of the globe; France floundered. Then America, using private firms at first, tackled the job; but they, too, met with many obstacles and nearly abandoned the project. But instead of being allowed to give up on it as a good business would when costs exceed investments, the federal government, under Theodore Roosevelt, got into the picture. It didn't simply farm out the job now—which, in light of the enormous expense involved, would have courted another failure. No, it assigned it to the Army Corp of Engineers and placed a general in charge of the project. The workers, many hundreds of whom already perished when the French made their attempts, were now forced to do their work under orders of the commander in chief of the American military.

The story is the same elsewhere, including the flight industry—where government-run airports have been the source of much consternation both for environmentalists and for those with different visions as to how that industry might and should have developed.

Many of the activists concerned about wildlife preservation and conservation are not champions of large alterations of the environment, such as the building of huge dams or the rerouting of rivers, accomplished for the sake of making various places inhabitable and exploitable by human beings. Although there are many friends of the TVA, most environmentalists are not among them. The same goes for the Hoover Dam and the massive irrigation systems achieved from the colossal rerouting of rivers.

And while one point of this book is to champion rather than denigrate revisions of the environment that make human life better, some projects that aim at this goal can be ill advised, likely to bring more grief than joy, especially in the long run.

The likelihood increases when governments deploy their customary tool—coercive force—in pursuit of the desired goals. In that case, rational reservations can be swept aside in a way that just isn't possible when the cooperation of all relevant parties can be obtained only by voluntary agreement.

The private sector is naturally restrained by the fact that investors and businesspeople working only with their own money cannot embark on projects that are financially futile and highly risky in other ways as well. Sadly, though, as a general rule most members of the environmental movement prefer to let big government handle the job of caring for the environment. For whatever reasons, they have no confidence in private sector solutions. Yet the only way that some of these mammoth projects that have carved up the world could have been carried out is by enlisting the power of governments. Only governments have the power to conscript unwilling labor and expropriate private property—not only in the form of taxes but also in the form of land via eminent domain. Thus, it is only governments that engage in routine rampages against the wilds.

A balanced approach to treating the wilds—to taming only those parts that are reasonably needed by human beings, as and when they need them—is to leave the matter to voluntary methods and keep the government out of it, except insofar as it needs to be enlisted to protect property rights.

THE PRACTICE OF INDIVIDUALIST ENVIRONMENTALISM

What does an individualist environmentalism imply in practice? The main implication is that many realms now under public supervision should be transferred to the private sector. Private property rights must be firmly established and protected within the legal system. Trespassing on private property must be promptly and justly punished. There must be no toleration of freewheeling negative externalities—that is, of bad, costly, but avoidable side effects—however much clamoring for them on grounds of special privilege exists in the political arena.

In the few spheres where it is technically impossible to discern distinct domains, so that laws against trespass are inapplicable, personal injury laws will have to be applied. To pollute the air mass, for example, constitutes injury to innocent third parties and must, therefore, not be tolerated on grounds of some kind of social cost–benefit accounting. Individuals matter most, not social aggregates "as a whole."

This approach could make serious improvements in the environment and encourage balance of the ecosystem. Some transitional problems will, of course, have to be faced. Some past collectivization and the resulting tragedies of commons cannot be undone. But better late than never. As Terry Anderson and Donald Leal put it,

> People are beginning to realize that markets can be a powerful force in the environmental movement. Market-based incentives have become a common approach in both the private and public sectors. Corporations are searching for ways to increase profits in environmentally friendly ways. Policymakers are facing the reality that a cleaner environment comes at an increasingly higher cost.[19]

There is evidence for the environmental benefits of markets all around us but, perhaps, most clearly in the contrast between what Soviet-style socialist central planning has done to the environment in eastern Europe and the comparatively less harmful results arising from the far more capitalist, free-market, private property–based system of the West. But my point here is not so much to rely on such a historical record. It is to suggest that such an approach (resting as it does on the political and legal implications of classical individualism[20]) is more in line with the nature of reality. And that should be the central concern of environmentalists—to urge the adjustment of human choices, actions, and institutions to the nature of our world.

Environmentalists need to be more optimistic about the prospects of managing environmental problems in a legal framework of individual liberty. What many in the environmental movement fail to realize (or, perhaps, to admit) is that the environmental problems that can be clearly identified rather than merely speculated about are generated by the tragedy of the commons. They are not generated by the privatization of resources or by the implementation of the principles that prohibit dumping and other kinds of trespassing, principles derived from an individualist conception of justice and proper public policy.

With more attention to protecting individual rights to life, liberty, and property, there would be fewer human-created ecological problems.[21] The necessary costs attending the benefits of human exploitation of the environment would be perceived more clearly and dealt with more forthrightly. The environment would be happier, but, more important, we humans would be happier, too.

This does not mean that advocates of private property and markets can promise an untroubled, blissful Elysium. Of course there are environmental problems to which solutions are difficult even to imagine. Even if one particular country has managed to institute the legal/constitutional measures that would best handle environmental problems, the international arena may lag. Various problems of judicial inefficiency, the tragedy of the commons, political deadlocks, and the like will continue to permeate the international public realm.

We must always keep in mind that the exact nature of private property rights, and hence the legal issues surrounding their protection and disposition, will often depend on just what exactly is being owned. These matters usually get worked out best in local adjudication, not broad national legislation that pretends to a knowledge of local conditions the law crafters lack. Obviously, some stuff is very difficult to own in quite the way one owns a clearly bounded physical entity like a house, dresser, or car—waterways and air masses, for example, present special issues and difficulties.

The incremental development of property law can accommodate these special difficulties just as it accommodates new technological developments. When it comes to environmental matters, the right to private property must always be the default position, any refinement of or departure from which must be made in light of real and existing difficulties. Such refinements or departures are well advised only within very specific contexts and cannot be treated as the baseline or standard model for treating very different cases.

There are issues of a more global import. The destruction of the ozone layer, if it were a real prospect, would be a threat to virtually everyone, yet it is at present uncertain whether human beings are responsible for it—there are, after all, natural causes involved. If it should turn out that certain kinds of human activities do cause this damage and if harm to human beings will be the result, those activities may be curtailed or even prohibited. After all, no one may place poison in the atmosphere with impunity, and the problem with the ozone layer is not unlike that—the destruction of something that is not anyone's property and thus no one's to destroy at will, while it, nonetheless, serves to do harm to individuals. However, the evidentiary basis for blaming human activity is very far from established.

Another problem that's hard to solve without the relevant scientific evidence is the destruction of the Amazonian rain forest, in this case by persons—or, rather, governments. Here, too, the only point that can be made is that if it is demonstrated that this destruction would injure others who have not consented to be so treated, the process must be legally stopped. The reason is, once again, that if one even unintentionally but knowingly violates the rights of others, the action can be a kind of negligent assault or even homicide. If, then, cutting down the trees in the Amazonian rain forest can be shown to uniquely result in the destruction of the lives and properties of others, this can be just cause for legally prohibiting it.

Of course, when there are no proper institutional instruments—that is, a constitution of natural human individual rights—to guard against such actions, it is difficult to suggest where one should turn. The most effective approach in these kinds of cases would be to tie various diplomatic negotiations— including military cooperation, bank credit, and cultural exchanges—to terms that would effectively express the principles of private property rights. The quid pro quo approach might be utilized on numerous fronts—including in the drafting of treaties—and once the principles and terms have been firmly entrenched, even military action might be justified when environmental destruction occurs on a massive enough scale. Consider that if Brazil wishes to maintain friendly relations with the United States or some other neighboring country and this other country's legal system firmly acknowledges the environmental implications of the private property rights system, such friendly relations would have to be manifest in part by Brazil's compliance with the international implications of such a system. This would apply even if Brazil itself does not adhere to such legal measures within its own borders.[22]

The principle is similar to that of other international agreements by which countries commit themselves to legal measures vis-à-vis citizens and organizations of other countries that they do not observe within their own borders. Trade agreements, contract laws, and numerous economic regulations bind foreign nationals in their interaction with a given country's population, even if within the foreign national's country itself these do not apply. The same kind of restrictions could be achieved on the environmental front.

We may now return to the more general implications of the private property rights approach to managing environmental problems. For one, we must acknowledge that in some cases protecting the rights of individuals in this strict manner may lead to their not enjoying certain benefits that they might have regarded as even greater than the benefit of not suffering the harm caused by, say, pollution.

But this is not relevant. The just treatment of individuals must respect their autonomy and their choice in judging what they think is best for themselves, even if and when they are mistaken, as long as this does not involve violating the rights of others. Paternalism and consistent capitalism are incompatible political ideals! The system of rights that grounds the legal framework that supports a consistent individualist-capitalism is sound, if it is, precisely because as a system of laws it is the one that is most respectful of individual rights—that is, it rests on the acknowledgment of the sovereignty of individual human beings.

This general virtue shows equal respect for every person

who embarks on social life, and it is this equal respect for all that justifies the establishment of legal protection for all—even if such a system does not guarantee that everyone will in fact make the most of its provisions. Nor does it guarantee that all values sought by members of human communities would be best secured via such a system. For example, technological progress in space travel might be enhanced by not paying heed to the strict liability provisions of the natural rights individualist legal system. But that does not mean that rights, liability, due process, and other principles that protect the lives of all members of a society should be chucked whenever they prove to be inconvenient to someone.

In short, the ultimate objective of such a system is a form of justice—not welfare, not progress, not equality of condition, not artistic advancement, even though these and many other values are abetted by a system of justice. A just social system must uphold and respect every person's status as a being with dignity, that is, as a being with the freedom and the responsibility to achieve a morally excellent life in his or her own case.

A BROADER VIEW OF NATURE

It might be a good idea to step back for a bit and consider how the voluntary relations that characterized the human free market can be paralleled in the natural world. It's not always dog eat dog (though I've never seen a dog eat a dog, come to think of it!). Just as human relations are various and multifaceted, so are relations between humans and the natural world. Humans prey on animals and exploit natural resources, just as other animals do, and there's nothing wrong with that. But human beings and other creatures also enjoy many mutual beneficial relationships, and these are part of the environmental picture, too.

Many animals and plants live in what is called a "commensal" fashion. That is, some of them feed on or otherwise gain benefits from the activities of others without depriving their hosts of anything at all. Commensalism is, thus, distinguished from parasitism, whereby some animals feed off the bodies of others in a way that deprives these others of something valuable.

Commensal relations also obtain between human and nonhuman animals. Beneath Paris, for example, the African cricket thrives because of the warmth the subway streets provide. In Rome, there are millions of starlings that come to benefit from the heat generated in the center of the city. They do produce the considerable inconvenience of tons of droppings, but it appears the human population has learned to live with this. Venice has become a veritable jungle in which seagulls prey on pigeons—helpfully lured onto the battlefield by humans spreading bread crumbs. We know that dogs and cats have it pretty easy thanks to us. In exchange for a little companionship, they get free room and board. There are probably a great many more commensual relations between human beings and other animals that simply go unreported.

Arguably, a form of commensalism is evident in the marketplace too, as when the establishment of one business gives rise to other, adjacent ones that benefit from yet take nothing from the first. If some big firm opens a plant in a neighborhood, other, smaller firms often start up around it. Perhaps the most conspicuous example is that of concessionaires at sports and entertainment events. Nothing is taken from the big firm in the process.

This commensal relationship may be an alternative to what

many see as an allegedly zero-sum relationship of the market-place whereby the gain of some must involve the loss of others. Indeed, a great many people see the marketplace as a kind of boxing ring so that for one to win, another must lose. In fact, the marketplace is much more akin to an endless marathon race in which there is a long span of often changing positions, with some even attaching themselves to others, we might say "commensally," so as to follow the right pace at which to proceed or to shield oneself from a head wind.

Maybe even the public goods problem can be understood a bit better by analogy to commensalism. If some folks pay for a service from which others can benefit, if the former were motivated to do so before others, these others can benefit without the former abandoning their pursuits. Thus, if it is of value to me to give to a charity, others could just lay back, refusing to contribute or contribute as much as I do. Or in purchasing some goods or services, there is often what people call the free-rider problem, namely, that others will gain from my investment. In the case of radio broadcasts by what are called listener-supported stations, this is supposed to be the problem. Yet, in fact, I and millions of others can and often do support such projects, knowing full well that others will benefit and that we could, too, without making any contribution if they gave their support. But the value that I and other devotees gain is great enough for us not to care much about the fact that others, too, will benefit from our obtaining it. And this seems to be a widespread approach, nothing idiosyncratic.

The public goods and free-rider problems arise from a misconception of human motivation. They assume that everyone is focused completely and exclusively on wringing every penny out of an opportunity, even if this obsessive pursuit kills the chances of reaching the initial goal one was pursuing.

Some people fit the picture. Certainly not everyone does, however. Most folks do not mind commensal relationships, so they do not feel the need to attempt to cash in on every benefit they confer on others, as long as they do gain those benefits they are seeking. Good-looking women might try to charge the men ogling them but don't. Architects might try to charge members of a community for the beauty they confer on a neighborhood, but they don't.

It seems that the commensalism we find in the wild has an imperfect but useful analogue in society. We can—though we often do not because of certain human attributes such as jealousy and envy not shared with other animals—enjoy benefits from what others do, even if indirectly, by piggybacking on their efforts and gaining opportunities in the meantime. But by failing to consider this as one of the ways human beings make out in a free society, there is a lot of nonsense going around about exploitation and free riding, casting aspersions on the marketplace instead of recognizing its superiority to alternative ways of organizing human economic affairs.

Underlying the suspicion of the marketplace is the view that only those human relations are worthwhile that have as their motivation to benefit others. If I merely benefit others inadvertently, indirectly, that is not good enough. There may be something to this when it comes to close relationships, friendship, familial bonds, and so forth. I am supposed to actively want to help my friends, not just benefit them incidentally.

Fortunately, the invisible hand of Adam Smith, the free marketplace, makes much of this consternation about helping people moot. We do it even when we do not think about it. The world of commerce, as of most other things, is not a zero-sum arena. We need not accept the judgment of the likes of Peter Singer, who advises us that only altruistic behavior toward animals is morally commendable.

WHAT COMES FIRST

What I have tried to show in this chapter is that, at least when it comes to the environment, conflict between individual rights and human community values is only apparent. And this should not be surprising. What is unique about human beings is that we are free, rational, and creative living entities; but, just like many other living beings, we also flourish best in communities rather than in isolation. Indeed, the company of others will nearly always be potentially beneficial to human beings and thus is consonant with and expressive of our nature. The individualism that stresses the need for choice and, thus, for individual rights must be seen not as an obstacle to but as a necessary condition for healthy community living.

The human capacity for thought and choice is, however, more fundamental to our nature and thus to our well-being than membership in communities. This is because it is only by observing, conceptualizing, evaluating, and making choices that a human being can distinguish between good and bad communities to begin with. And that choice is certainly vital. The rejection of a communist, fascist, authoritarian, or other tyrannical community must be seen as a crucial capacity for a human being, indeed, one that each person ought to exercise. In such cases, where a conflict between community and the individual arises, clearly the rights of the individual are morally prior, even if in certain cases individuals will exercise these rights wrongly, badly. Even then, the fact that they have made a choice remains what is vital about their humanity. Other animals, too, flourish in communities, but only human beings must flourish by choice.

The example of environmental challenge to individualism is important because here we have what seemed, at first blush, to be a clear demonstration of the need to reject individual rights in favor of community values. But that conflict turned out to be bogus. Given the nature of human life—its naturalism and individualism—the individual rights approach is indispensable in dealing with any of the problems surrounding human affairs. And the management of the problems of human community life, including environmental problems, is no exception to this vital principle.

One cannot demand the impossible. For too long, demands placed on the fields of morality and politics have been unjustly severe: final, irrefutable, timeless answers were sought, and in response to the inevitable failure to produce these invulnerable final answers, cynicism about the prospects of any workable answers has gained a foothold throughout the intellectual community as well as among members of the general public. As a result, many assume that no solid intellectual solution to any of the value-oriented areas of human problems can be reached. On this assumption, the best we can expect is some kind of consensus that vaguely represents the tastes and preferences of a significant number of the concerned population. Yet this "consensus" is a house of cards. Tastes and preferences are unstable, flexible, and so hard to determine that the only thing that emerges from the flux is some kind of arbitrary public policy produced by bureaucrats or by dictators. But human nature is enduring. And so human life and human community involve certain lasting principles, too. Taking those into account, we can fruitfully approach the many problems that confront us.

Pollution is a relatively recent problem, one that proves to be an important, difficult test of political theories. Collectivist systems, such as fascism, socialism, and even the welfare state, gauge the justice of the state by reference to considerations that are, in the last analysis, unnatural: some idea of a common purpose to be served that may cancel out the rights of human individuals. By contrast, individualism and its political economic system, capitalism, stress the ultimate importance of the rights and value of the individual, gauging the acceptability of public policies by their success in protecting individual human rights.

In this discussion, I have considered the extremely different views of socialist and capitalist, collectivist and individualist, or libertarian and communitarian positions as manifesting archetypically opposing views on the environment and, by implication, all problems of human community life. No doubt, there are watered-down versions of each of these that we could examine, although that approach does not lend itself to systematic treatment. And when we are considering a political–economic system, we are dealing with the most general principles that ought to govern community life even if, for some perhaps even valid reasons, the principles of the systems under inspection might need to be adapted to accommodate special circumstances. I do not deny for a moment that actual community life is far more a matter of a many shades of gray than simple black and white, to quote one early referee of this chapter. But it is also true that without a clear idea of what counts as black and what counts as white, the various shades of gray could not even be identified.

No sane political theorist holds that some system of political ideas and ideals will be adhered to perfectly, without exception, should the public become convinced of the worth of what he or she proposes. It is, for example, clear that Socrates created his ideal polity "in speech" only, not as an actual community. Even the less idealistically oriented political theorists have usually realized that when optimal standards of justice are developed, it takes nearly impossible measures of human vigilance to sustain them in practice. Nevertheless, it is vital that the standards be identified. It is to that end that I have advanced my ideas here, testing them against what most people would recognize as a challenging case.

My thesis is, admittedly, radical. It envisions only human beings as owners while leaving much of the rest of nature as subject to ownership. This should not be surprising since it is human beings who are the only species in nature known to us to require moral space, a sphere of authority wherein they can interact with nature to the exclusion of others who would, were they to intrude, subvert the moral independence and responsibility of the victim. The system of private property that my thesis embraces is one that facilitates individual moral and legal accountability. Of course, securing realms of individual responsibility will not guarantee the optimal outcome. Yet the pressure to do the right thing is greater when one must carry the burden of having done the wrong thing.

In our age of so-called postmodernism, it may seem odd that someone proposes that a crucial element of modernity—the recognition of the essential individuality of human beings—be affirmed both philosophically and politically and that a rational, objective system of principles can be developed on its basis. It seems that in our time, many thinkers are discouraged about the challenges this kind of a recommendation poses in ethics, law, and diplomacy. Some have become nihilists in the face of those challenges. Lacking criteria for judgments in any domain, they embraced wholesale ambiguity, subjectivity, and, ultimately, the rule of brute force.

We must reject this sweeping skepticism and nihilism, embrace a more optimistic approach to public affairs, and apply it to environmental matters as well.

4

PUTTING HUMANS FIRST

S ad to say, some people do not put humans first. These people are not necessarily professional philosophers or animal
rights activists, either. Many in the general public seem to have
imbibed at least a watered-down version of the antihuman ani-
mus promoted by radical environmentalism.

A while ago, I visited a cousin who lives in Berlin, a
sprawling city being rebuilt after over forty years of socialist
devastation. What I remember most vividly is the profusion of
cranes all over the city, testifying to how much work needs to
be done to make the former socialist paradise into a user-
friendly city again.

My cousin, her husband, and their two young children live
in the former East Berlin in an apartment that still bears the
scars of socialist utilitarianism. Although now refurbished and
modernized, the place still has no elevator, so that whenever
they enter or leave the house, the kids must be hauled up and
down the stairs. Despite the relative compactness of nearly all
cars and the widespread use of bicycles, parking is a big problem. But the shops and restaurants of the city now have that

healthy look of abundance, with plenty to pick from and a charming atmosphere of gemütlichkeit.

Despite the undeniable evidence facing everyone who will but look, my cousin and those of her friends I met, all young ladies with toddlers, tend in their politics toward the Left. They champion the welfare state, even if it means forcing Germans to finance hundreds of social programs that they can hardly afford and that throw roadblocks in the way of the recovery. They are sympathetic to the Greens, anticapitalists who refuse to acknowledge that under their preferred socialist system of political economy, countries throughout the globe have suffered environmental destruction galore. The tragedy of the commons is an idea that isn't well grasped by most of the Greens I've encountered, not excluding my cousin and her friends.

To these young champions of the Green agenda, I made the mistake of admitting that, yes, back in the United States I own and drive a sport-utility vehicle (SUV), a vehicle that is the bane of all politically correct environmentalists everywhere. Without asking me anything, they declared my SUV ownership to be a crime, something on the order of a mortal sin. The discussion was good natured and friendly enough, but one could not accuse the ladies of open-mindedness on the subject. The verdict they passed on me was, guilty, beyond reasonable doubt, a verdict reached without any hint of due process.

What might such due process have consisted of? Well, for starters, a little inquiry into why I, in particular, own and drive my rather modest and, incidentally, small SUV. That would seem to have been the civilized thing to do prior to any categorical condemnation of me. Maybe knowing something of my two back operations would have been instructive. Maybe knowing where I live and what my transportation requirements are would have been useful as well.

After I sold my 1993 BMW, I had trouble getting into smaller cars, thanks to the two back operations and chronic neck pain. With the SUV, I can step up to my seat, and it no longer feels like I am scaling an obstacle on a Marine training course. Another mildly relevant fact is that the vehicle is rather small and consumes not what the SUV foes keep claiming, namely, ten to thirteen miles per gallon but eighteen to twenty-three miles per gallon. And then there's the fact that I live out in the country and like to bring supplies back home in bulk, not bit by bit—an efficiency that actually saves gas in the long run. And then again, the vehicle is safer than many others, and at my age I no longer feel invincible.

All these details (assuming one felt inclined to justify one's peaceful use of a legally owned vehicle to impertinently accusatory others) would seem to be relevant to the charge of gratuitous SUV usage. But no. When one is caught up in a simple, beautiful idea, one that is supposed to usher in universal happiness for us all, the trivial details of an actual human life with all its problems and goals are irrelevant. For the self-appointed guardians of the earth's welfare, "guilty until proven innocent" is the only way to mete out justice—never mind the welfare of the human individuals residing on that earth.

The kind of radical environmentalism that I have taken issue with in this book assumes that no improvement of the human lot can justify any alteration of nature in its wild state. The wilds, untouched by human intervention, are ipso facto a sacrosanct paradise. The value of the wilds is axiomatic, beyond question. Thus a road, parking lot, housing development, shopping mall, amusement park, or whatever else people might build to make life more interesting and enjoyable is necessarily a bad thing. Unless, of course, that enjoyment pertains to contemplating untouched nature—perhaps from the vantage point of an already built house or condo.

I live in a canyon. The canyons are very nice to look at. But that is also one reason why neither I nor anyone else ought to keep others out of them. Those of us who currently reside here do not possess any royal claim to our surroundings. Fellow canyon dweller Wayne Brown doesn't agree. He believes that he does have a God-given right or, at any rate, an environmentalism-given right, to live in his canyon without anyone else coming there to "rip up the land."

Is there any point to wondering how he could be living there himself without having ripped up the land for his own dwelling? But if the axioms of environmentalism don't need to be particularly logical or justifiable, perhaps neither do any blatant contradictions of them.

Appreciators of "nature"—actually the wilds because nature includes us all—like Mr. Brown believe that they not only own the 3,000 or 5,000 or 15,000 acres on which they happen to have built their homes but also have the right to rule any part of the surroundings they happen to like, even if they don't own it. Brown and his allies do not own the whole of Trabuco Canyon; they own a bit of land there. And now others would like to own a bit of land there as well. Well, what of it?

Of course, when new residents come to live in a place, they need to make sure that they, too, pay their way—for trash collection, water usage, and parking. Thus, an appropriate accommodation between the old residents and the new residents is established. But neither group ought to have the legal power to impose its wishes willy-nilly on the rest.

Without property rights that all are obliged to respect, we cannot live with each other in a civilized manner. We can behave only like a lynch mob, perhaps succeeding in imposing our particular wishes for the moment, until some other guy's mob grows bigger than our mob. Thus are humans reduced to pack animals. But we are better than that. We have the power to act rationally and with respect toward others. Mutual respect for human rights and aspirations is far more important to achieve than the maintenance of a view. And it gives us the best chance to improve our lives in all respects.

Such considerations are often alien to the environmentalist mentality. In the case of my SUV driving, it made no difference to my cousin and her friends what my needs and aspirations are, how I and my family might benefit from the vehicle. All that matters is that I am not following the environmental program.

In this respect, radical environmentalism is indeed a mere variant of the socialism the East Germans have presumably escaped. Each of these ideologies is a variant of collectivism, the notion that the individual counts for nothing when compared to the grandeur of some greater collective whole—whether that greater whole is Papa State or Mother Nature.

Are SUVs gas guzzling? It depends on what you want from them. It depends on who you are, what your priorities are. These are judgments for you alone to make, based on your own intimate knowledge of your own personal circumstances. It is impossible for central planners to tell from afar what kind of vehicle you should purchase or what sort of furniture or kitchenware. Yes, there is a public philosophy under which such remote judgments are deemed valid—and under which variations of personal values and personal circumstances are deemed irrelevant. Yesterday it was socialism. Today it's environmentalism.

Under any philosophy of collectivism, there is no acknowledgment of individuality. You and I and the rest of us are all merely cells in the body of society (or of nature), and we must conform to some grand overarching holistic plan. That is what makes collectivism so drastically different from the individualist system that is the inheritance of the United States.

But, of course, the individualist system is itself quite radical, given the history of tribal thinking that has dominated humanity for the bulk of its political existence. Even today—after the American founders have made so clear that we all have the right to our lives, our liberty, and our pursuit of happiness— Old World public philosophies persist. Intellectuals influenced by European thinking, according to which ethnic, national, and other groups tend to be of central importance rather than the individual—all want us to step in line with a one-size-fits-all way of life. Radical environmentalism is a mere offshoot or variant of this individual-squashing mentality.

IF LIFE IS WORTH LIVING, IS IT WORTH IMPROVING?

One ingredient of the environmentalist theology we must emphatically reject is the perverse insistence on reading human life out of the rest of nature—as if we human beings had been deposited into this reality by some runaway dump truck from another dimension.

In truth, we are every bit as natural as the ants, snail darters, spotted owls, or any resident of the wetlands. Indeed, we are the crown of creation, the highest level of nature attained thus far in the known universe. And this means that all the SUVs and airplanes and housing developments are a part of nature, too, as are bridges, disposable diapers, and nuclear waste.

Part of the rhetoric that gives environmentalism its pseudomoral nimbus concerns the supposed clash between precious nature and all that is artificial and technological, the lowly "man-made." We hear it all the time, as when the bass rumble of some nature program narrator explains how some part of nature has been spoiled by that most omnipresent of nemeses: "MAN"!

When a lion destroys a zebra, this isn't depicted as the tragic demise of a natural organism at the hands of an alien, unnatural force. When hurricanes, volcanoes, typhoons, or tornadoes wreak their havoc, these too are accepted as completely natural, if destructive, events (except when they are perversely attributed in some incomprehensible remote fashion to alleged human misconduct).

Yet we are as much a part of nature as those wetlands the environmentalists wish to shield from us. One is tempted to ask why they don't go out of their way to protect other parts of nature from, say, termites or floods. Why aren't they willing to ban from nature everything else that changes the environment surrounding it? But of course, every aspect of nature changes other parts of nature as a matter of course. The environmentalists are inconsistent because they have to be. Ecosystems are not static tableaus.

What is true is that human beings are a different kind of natural phenomenon from, say, volcanoes and foxes. But so what? Birds are different from fish, and fish are different from amoebas. So the fact that human beings are even very radically different from other species is by no means unprecedented and certainly not unnatural.

The rhetoric of environmentalism must be recast if it is to contribute intelligibly to debates about nature. Let's stop trying to exclude human life from the realm of nature. Then we can ask whether it is the right thing for us to build this house or dam, that parking lot, this nuclear power generator.

But until this change of heart happens, everything from SUVs, housing, and even cyberspace will continue to be routinely targeted by those who hate our uniquely human ability to rearrange our surroundings. If all we humans did was move branches around in a creek, like the beaver, the environmentalists would probably let us off the hook. But we do so much more than that to refashion our world. And the more we do, the more contempt we earn from the anti-innovators.

Consider the philosophy of Neil Postman of New York University, who once showed up on the PBS *NewsHour* talking about cyberspace. The professor's basic idea is simple: All advances in technology are a Faustian bargain. You never really win—you just swap one hardship for another. Says him, anyway.

The latest human-crafted affliction is the information superhighway. According to Postman, we all suffer isolation and alienation—an excess of individualism, really—when we use our computer to import the world outside. Sure, the ability to shop from home or research from home or teleconference from home might reduce traffic accidents or the risk of contact with communicable disease. It might permit a greater quantity of quality time with friends and family. The Internet might even enable easier and more frequent contact with people we know abroad but had to wait weeks to hear from in the past, and it may even encourage the writing skills of teens who so eagerly post e-mail to their friends around, yes, the entire globe. Talk about encouraging cross-cultural contact!

But none of these positives outweigh the downside, it seems. Professor Postman even blames the current widespread flirtation with tribalism, from Bosnia-Herzegovina to Canada, on this new technology! He suggests that far from dissolving borders, the global network drives us to once again seek solace in the tribe. (As if intellectuals haven't been pushing all manner of tribalism for umpteen centuries already.)

When Postman was asked what we should do to moderate

the bad impact of new technology, he answered, in part, with an example. He told of how he had once bought a car that came with the costly option of cruise control. He asked the dealer what this would achieve for him—what problem it would solve. When told that it would allow him to take his foot off the gas pedal, he noted that for thirty years he had managed to drive with his foot on the gas pedal. So what's the big deal?

Now, from this example we may conclude either that Mr. Postman doesn't care about cruise control or that there is never any net benefit from new technology, so who needs it? (One difficulty with the latter conclusion is that Postman does get around by car, not donkey.)

For my part, I was delighted when cruise control was introduced. I drive extensively and often take long trips with my children. I am always relieved to be able to take my foot off the pedal while driving along on the interstate highway system. When I got a good deal on a van without the cruise control, I had it installed in part because it keeps me driving close enough to the speed limit.

It seems incontrovertible that cruise control matters more to me that it matters to Professor Postman. Fleshing out the implications further, we may even say that particular technological innovations will survive in the market only if a sufficient number of people—whose judgments ought not to be demeaned out of hand—want to benefit from them. The fact that many new technologies do survive suggests that many people do like them and benefit from them.

Yet here is Professor Postman saying that because for him nothing is gained via cruise control, no one else gains from it, either. Never mind what the rest of us might have to report about our own experience. Professor Postman knows best!

Of course, I too drove for thirty years without cruise control and didn't suffer inordinately. No doubt, people live with headaches, backaches, bad teeth, dandruff, body odor, and all manner of hampering conditions without feeling compelled to forfeit life altogether. Millions of years went by without musical instruments, recorded sound, photographs, or even leather shoes—let alone the telephone or high-speed ambulance. But by Professor Postman's reckoning, we never made any gains at all. On his view, our lives are no better than that of the first bunch of people, those who lived for just twenty or thirty years in unvacuumed caves before being struck down by some now obscure disease.

There is something in the radical environmentalist and/or antitechnological view of the world that fosters resentment of human convenience, even joy, if that convenience and joy is man-made. I recently saw the movie *Divine Secrets of the Ya-Ya Sisterhood*, in which a mother and daughter persuade the pilot of a crop duster to take them on a riveting flight. The little plane took off and flew about so perkily, with everyone having such a good time experiencing the open air whooshing past them as they swooped up and down, that watching it, too, could only be a delight.

And I got to thinking about all those people who, if they were consistent in applying their environmentalist ideas, would condemn just this sort of exhilarating human adventure. Who needs planes, right, when you can walk? Why be technological when you can be "natural"? Why not just take a stroll in the woods or listen to the chirp of the birds or the rippling of the water in some creek? Or catch a glimpse of wild animals frolicking in the forest? But creating fierce flying machines and using them just to have fun—isn't that the height of self-indulgent hubris? Or so some folks would chide us.

Yet how wonderful is that imaginary plane ride! And how wonderful are all the millions of actual plane and train and automobile rides. It's great that we can indulge our human imagination and benefit from what our minds create.

Radical environmentalists, sadly, often seem to despise human beings and what we have created on this earth. Those bridges that span the rivers, those planes that take off at all the airports, those trains and cars and all the rest that use gasoline and require parts made from steel in soot-producing factories—all this infuriates them. Too bad. It's one thing to counsel prudence about how the wilds are treated, quite another to ooze contempt for the human way—the creative way—of dealing with the world.

There is no shame in being a human being. It's a *good* thing.

LIFE IS GOOD

Every year I resolve to ignore the doomsayers. I reason as follows. The news will always be driven by the scariest happenings, lest the viewer or reader go about his or her life happily with the limited awareness that is the lot of us all. The media need to put things out on a regular basis, so they have to stir up interest in what they offer. If people can be scared good and hard, instead of walking the dog they'll stay tuned, and the media makers will have their audience.

But there is another factor that feeds the frenzy of bad news: old age. I am rapidly becoming an old person myself, so I know whereof I speak.

Thing is, it is very tempting for the old, who tend to lose some of their pep and who face an ever more abbreviated future, to project what they go through onto the world around them. Ergo, everything is getting worse. It's not just their own health, love life, social relations, or job security that is slowly shriveling. No, it's the world itself that is disintegrating and collapsing.

Of course, there is much real bad news about the state of today's world. On the other hand, there are libraries of books from every conceivable era of human history in which other old folks from these other eras also report how the world of their own day is going to hell, how morality is no more, how people are no longer nice or hardworking or honest or decent or civil, and so forth. Each age is freighted with these laments. And yet it seems to me that many things are much better for most of us alive today than they were for the Joes and Janes of neolithic times.

I recently attended a conference in New York City at which some very eminent scholars kept repeating the same gloomy refrain. Our age is doomed, art is doomed, science is doomed—in short, humanity is doomed. A great many prominent environmentalists, of course, make a living out of telling us how rotten we have been and continue to be and how we'll meet our doom. Social engineers are doomsayers, too, partly to improve the demand for their services as improvers of the human condition. And politicians campaign endlessly on the theme that all those in Washington are immoral or amoral knaves and that we need to clean house if there is to be any hope.

Sure, we love to scare ourselves to death. It's very dramatic. But at the same time, there are always those old folks about who find the later years of life understandably bleak and who, instead of making the most of what is left for them, blame their plight on the universe at large. But the universe is fine. It may be gradually running down, but it has billions of years left to go.

Mind you, I have nothing against careful criticism or seeking improvement where it is genuinely needed. But all this sweeping doom and gloom about human life in general is just not credible. Sure, my life may have some lamentable features as my journey to the grave accelerates, but this is not the prospect that faces my kids in the near future. They have a good chance of making a decent world for themselves, and they could use some reminder of that. Their own decrepitude and senescence won't commence for decades.

I am an optimist. I try keep my eyes and ears open, and what I perceive confirms my optimism.

Over the years, I have been a student of philosophy, reading some of the most exciting products of the human mind—as well as some of the most depressing products—to great profit. I have also found fiction to be extremely rewarding. The addiction began when I was only eight or nine and devoured Hungarian translations of works by Mark Twain, Earle Stanley Gardner, Zane Gray, Max Brand, Karl May, and half a dozen others. I would read into the wee hours of the night, huddled under my blankets with a flashlight so as to escape my mother's wrath for not getting enough sleep. To this day, no matter how full of tasks and challenges and complications my life is, I continue to read novels by David Lodge, Winston Graham, W. Somerset Maugham, Thomas Mann, Graham Greene, Margaret Drabble, Barbara Pym, Mark Saltzman, and many others.

My mother also used to drag me to classical concerts back in my early years. While I mostly fell asleep—having spent the night reading—these, too, showed me some astonishing samples of human creativity. Then came the theater, art museums and galleries, jazz and the blues, and all the rest—malls and amusement parks, deserts, the sea and the mountains, night-clubs and promenades, and friends, lovers, colleagues, and, especially, my kids—all the endless good things in life that tend to persuade one that life *is* pretty darn good, all things considered.

No, I wasn't lucky enough to miss the horrors. I was born just six months before the outbreak of World War II and lived the first years of my life smack dab in the middle of it, with bombs falling around me, sirens going off all hours of the day and night, in a city in near total ruin and lives destroyed or maimed. I could not avoid seeing the evil of which human beings are capable. And then living under the brutal communists and growing up with a similarly brutal Nazi father certainly put me on notice about how rotten things can get. I have had my share of pain and disease and calamity and guilt—so I wouldn't say I have a Pollyanna view of life.

But all in all, life is good! There is no reason to dismiss the potential of our time on earth as cavalierly as so many earnest and profound—pretentious?—folks too often do. This insistence of some that the modern era is especially cruddy, soulless, shallow, and dead—what baloney! All this contempt for bourgeois values by intelligentsia Left and Right is just out to lunch, as far as I'm concerned. It's like, talk to the hand, because the face ain't listening.

Do they ever listen to music, look at paintings, attend plays, or read books? Don't they see the wonders of the human capacity to create, how it has filled the world with beauty?

We don't know directly what it was like in A.D. 300 or 1400, but we do have access to the testimony of residents of those eras. And, all in all, I do not get the impression that those ages were so fabulous, comparatively speaking. Yes, the twentieth century suffered some of the worst manifestations of human evil, and much of it is going on right now. Human choice produces both good and bad in the world.

Yet I do not believe that in our time evil has conquered. If you do believe it, I recommend taking a closer look. Read, listen, look, and, above all, do something interesting and valuable! If there is too little good in the world, make more.

WONDROUS HUMANITY

In the May 15, 2003, issue of the *New York Review of Books*, Peter Singer assesses the state of animal liberation thirty years after his cover article for the *Review* on the topic. I remember the article well. Interestingly, Singer quotes from that essay just the passage that I focused on in my second book,[1] although, of course, Singer hasn't deigned to address my critical response to him in that early book or my later discussion of animal rights.[2]

The passage in question is very revealing. Singer could not promise that "we will become healthier, or enjoy life more, if we cease exploiting animals. Animal Liberation will require greater altruism on the part of mankind than any other liberation movement, since animals are incapable of demanding it for themselves, or of protesting against their exploitation by votes, demonstration, or bombs."[3]

Singer goes on to ask, rhetorically one may assume, whether "man is capable of such genuine altruism? Who knows? If this book does have a significant effect, however, it will be a vindication of all those who have believed that man has within himself the potential for more than cruelty and selfishness."[4]

In my own book, I have indicated why the altruism Singer demands is misguided. It should not even be attempted— which isn't to say that decency and consideration toward animals are not part of a good human being's character. Clearly they are. But there is nothing wrong with pursuing happiness, either—there is nothing wrong with looking out for ourselves and exploiting nature, including animals, accordingly. Humans are more important, even better, than other animals, and we deserve the benefits that exploiting animals can provide.

What do we mean by "altruism"? According to one writer, "'Altruism' [is] *assuming* a duty to relieve the distress and promote the happiness of our fellows. . . . [To advocate altruism is to] maintain quite simply that a man may and should discount altogether his own pleasure or happiness as such when he is deciding what course of action to pursue."[5] Altruism means self-sacrifice. So what is called for, if we believe Singer, is not merely humane treatment of members of the nonhuman animal world but, literally, human self-sacrifice. Only for someone who has a very low estimate of the kind of self that is to be sacrificed would this appear to be a morally good thing. Indeed, the idea is contrary to living nature.

Why happiness is worth promoting for others but not for ourselves is unclear; are these others allowed to accept the happiness we produce for them, or must they, in turn, also think only of others and not of themselves? In any case, for Singer it isn't even this usual version of altruism that should guide us— that is, one that takes it that everyone ought to look out for other *human beings* first. For Singer, altruism requires that we take other animals as our priority as we conduct ourselves in our lives. We're suppose to sacrifice our well-being for the sake of the guppies and lizards.

The notion can be rendered semipalatable only by positing a choice between this kind of altruism and "cruelty and selfishness," that is, the kind of selfishness we have in mind when we speak of people who inflict needless pain and suffering just to be mean. But that's a false dichotomy. It also reveals a misanthropy that could be based only on the hasty generalization that because some people are evil, all people must be unworthy. As W. H. Auden once quipped, "We are here on earth to do good for others. What the others are here for, I don't know."[6] For most people, that reply may well be sufficient—it certainly cuts to the marrow of the matter. For those of us who want to think through the issues of life more thoroughly, this book has sought to answer the challenge of those who would place animals above human beings.

The most amazing feature of reality we have encountered so far is ourselves. What else in nature reflects on itself, creates and destroys to unheard of degrees, blames and praises its own kind, and even endlessly debates whether all this is routine or extraordinary?

We are, certainly, an unusual species. No other animal is quite like us, no matter how amazing or beautiful or dangerous it may be. Darwin, after all, was a human being who exemplified that which is unique and amazing about us, as do those of his followers who take him to have disputed the uniqueness of human beings. That uniqueness consists precisely in our enormous intellectual creativity. To be delighted at being human, one need not take irrational pride in the achievements of other human beings—the Aristotles, Mozarts, Einsteins, Edisons, van Goghs, Dostoyevskys, or John Glenns and Buzz Aldrins—as if we had done their deeds ourselves. Yet everyone, at the same time, is justified in admiring the human species, in delighting in all that human beings have done to earn a special place in the animal world.

It is a paradox of our intellectual capacity that so many of us use it to denigrate that very capacity. We are said to be too arrogant, too prideful and hubristic, too "speciesist." Our uniqueness and glorious potential is supposed to be a source not of joy but of sorrow. The arts are replete with examples of such grandiose self-denigration. And in philosophy, as well as such allied disciplines as evolutionary biology, psychology, and sociology, it is notorious how much gloom is produced, warning what a high a price we will pay for it all.

I do not wish to wantonly hurt other animals, and I consider those who do to be morally flawed. But I also consider those who wish to wantonly instill guilt in us for being glad of our humanity to be morally flawed. And I find their morality of altruism to be both insidious and perverse.

Yet even such misguided griping is quintessentially and uniquely human. Even as the fundamental distinctiveness of human beings is being denied, those doing the denying thereby exhibit it. They themselves direct themselves rather diligently and competently to the end of "demonstrating" not that we are really free to do and be as we choose but rather that our conscious will is an illusion. In other words, they exhibit the free will and conceptual ability to argue as they like.

Despite their protestations, however, it is a fact that our moral nature makes us unique. And if rights are conceptually tied to this fact, the ascription of rights to human animals but not to nonhuman animals is clearly warranted.

Not all the implications of our moral nature are elevating. We have the power to conduct ourselves badly. We can mistreat the environment and the lower animals. We can use them in ways that are not consistent with any rational purpose of our own.

But this is not to deny that we should put humans first and pursue our true interests diligently. It merely means that we should do so rationally, with prudence and care.

NOTES

INTRODUCTION

1. A similar issue arises vis-à-vis the ban on the use of DDT; for details on how it has contributed to human disease and death, see the Africa Fighting Malaria website, www.fightingmalaria.org/fighting_malaria.htm.

2. On the issue of eating—and feeding—meat, for which it is often necessary to kill animals, see Michael Martin, "A Critique of Moral Vegetarianism," *Reason Papers*, no. 3 (fall 1976): 13–43. It is worth asking the rhetorical question, If animals have the same rights human beings do, and this is a reason why it is not only morally wrong but to be prohibited to kill nonhuman animals, what is one to make of all the killing nonhuman animals do? After all, if they are indistinguishable from human beings in having rights, would this not imply they are also indistinguishable in having obligations to respect the rights of rights-bearing others? Are they then to be blamed and even prosecuted when they kill other nonhuman (and even human) animals? Ought their killings to be condemned and even forcibly stopped by legal authorities, just as the killings of humans by humans is to be, whenever that is possible?

CHAPTER 1

1. The most respected philosophical defenders of legal protection of animal rights or liberation are Tom Regan, *The Case for Animal Rights* (Berkeley:

University of California Press, 1983), and Peter Singer, *Animal Liberation* (New York: Hearst Corporation, 1991). Their arguments differ, Regan defending rights on grounds of a neo-Kantian understanding of the implications of animal consciousness, Singer defending liberation on grounds of utilitarian concerns for including animal experience as part of the calculus of pleasure and suffering.

2. Quoted in Michael Specter, "The Extremist," *The New Yorker*, April 14, 2003, 58.

3. Henry S. Salt, *Animals' Rights* (London: George Bell, 1892; Clark Summit, Pa.: Society for Animal Rights, 1980). This is perhaps the major philosophical effort to defend animal rights prior to Tom Regan's treatise on the topic.

4. See Charles Darwin, *The Descent of Man*, chaps. 3 and 4, reprinted in *Animal Rights and Human Obligations*, ed. Tom Regan and Peter Singer (Englewood Cliffs, N.J.: Prentice Hall, 1976), 72–81.

5. On these points, both the deontologically oriented Regan and the utilitarian-leaning Peter Singer tend to agree, although they differ considerably in their arguments.

6. Peter Singer holds that "we would be on shaky grounds if we were to demand equality for blacks, women, and other groups of oppressed humans while denying equal consideration to nonhumans" ("All Animals are Equal," in Regan and Singer, eds., *Animal Rights*, 150).

7. Tom Regan contends that "[it] is not to say that practices that involve taking the lives of animals cannot possibly be justified. . . . In order seriously to consider approving such a practice [it] would [have to] prevent, reduce, or eliminate a much greater amount of evil" ("Do Animals Have a Right to Life?" in Regan and Singer, eds., *Animal Rights*, 203–4).

8. Regan, *The Case for Animal Rights*.

9. Les Burwood and Ros Wyeth, "Ethics and the Vegan Way of Life," *Philosophers' Magazine*, November/December 1998, 19–22.

10. Burwood and Wyeth, "Ethics and the Vegan Way of Life," 21.

11. Robert Nozick, *Anarchy, State, and Utopia* (New York: Basic, 1974), 54.

12. John Hospers, "Review of *The Case for Animals Rights*," *Reason Papers*, no. 10 (fall 1985): 123.

13. Specter, "The Extremist," 56.

14. Specter, "The Extremist," 56. Specter says this is what "[Newkirk] told me, in the most unequivocal terms" (57–58).

15. Here and there, intimations of something like moral awareness are in evidence, as when great apes mourn a death among them or seem to chide

youngsters for being too uppity. Yet much of this hinges on a proclivity of researchers to anthropomorphize the wild animal world, thus putting the attribution in serious doubt.

A similar argument to that based on some resemblance between nonhuman animal and human behavior, though couched in the language of the biological and physiological sciences, concerns the fact that humans and chimps share 99.4 percent of their DNA. Based on this fact, a team of scientists led by Professor Morris Goodman at the Wayne State University School of Medicine has even proposed that chimps be classified as humans. "We humans appear as only slightly remodeled chimpanzee-like apes" ("Chimp Change: Experts Want to Add Primate to Human Class," Associated Press, *Orange County Register*, May 20, 2003, 9).

If classification were based on such percentiles, perhaps the thesis would be credible, but consider that we classify the world on the basis of a great many other factors than possession of DNA. Musicians are distinct from film directors not because they are different in possessing numbers of DNA but because of what they do. Chimps may be very close to humans as far as sharing DNA, but as far as what they are capable of doing, there is hardly any comparison. Just consider, the Associated Press didn't report on studies done by chimps on humans but the other way around, and that is enormously significant.

16. This is such a widely understood point that even those who dispute it abide by it. When others mischaracterize antiessentialists such as Richard Rorty as proponents of views they do not actually hold, they protest the mischaracterization just as if characterizations ought to be made in terms that conform to the essentials of what is being propounded. Any argument can be distorted by focusing on peripheral or "borderline" aspects and treating these "borderline cases" as if they were the central thrust or "normal case" of the argument.

17. Bernard E. Rollin, *Animal Rights and Human Morality* (Buffalo, N.Y.: Prometheus, 1981), 4.

18. Not all the suffering by animals used for scientific research, food, and sport chronicled by Tom Regan, Peter Singer, PETA, the Humane Society of the United States, and others is needed to secure the completely valid goals humans have with animals. So, the headway PETA has made with, for example, Burger King and McDonald's Corporation can thus be seen as quite laudable without embracing anything like the fiction of animal rights, however much rhetorical and public relations advantage there may be from deploying such a concept, given how much good work it has managed to do vis-à-vis the liberation of human beings across the globe. There may even be truth to the sociological claim that for such headway to occur, some have to exagger-

ate the moral case in behalf of how we ought to treat animals, although the risk of a backlash—in the form of a complete rejection of those claims by millions who have a good sense of just how much of a trick there is in it—cannot be ignored, either. In any case, the point here isn't the effectiveness of various tactics for achieving the goals of zealots, some of whom no doubt have transferred a sentimental attachment to animals to a global "philosophy." The point here is whether animals have rights, which they do not, beyond any reasonable doubt.

19. I discuss some of this in Tibor R. Machan, *Private Rights and Public Illusions* (New Brunswick, N.J.: Transaction, 1995).

20. See Richard Rorty, *Objectivity, Relativism, and Truth* (Cambridge: Cambridge University Press, 1991).

CHAPTER 2

1. From Albert Schweitzer, *Out of My Life and Thought*; available at http://www.hummingbirdworld.com/spiritnature/Schweitzer.htm (accessed August 25, 2003).

2. From *The Animal World of Albert Schweitzer*, ed. Charles Joy; available at http://www.saveourstrays.com/reverenc.htm (accessed August 25, 2003).

3. From *The Animal World of Albert Schweitzer*.

4. "Individual" need not mean "atomistic, isolated, antisocial, or asocial" individual. Such a characterization begs the question of what kind of individual we are faced with. For a detailed discussion of the type of individual a human being is, see Tibor R. Machan, *Capitalism and Individualism: Reframing the Argument for the Free Society* (New York: St. Martin's, 1990).

A different sort of defense of anthropocentrism is advanced in Thomas Palmer, "The Case for Human Beings," *The Atlantic*, no. 269 (January 1992): 83–88. Palmer notes that "in fact Homo sapiens is the crown of creation, if by creation we mean the explosion of earthly vitality and particularity long ago ignited by a weak solution of amino acids mixing in sunlit waters" (p. (88). Unfortunately, Palmer does not emphasize enough this feature of particularity in his defense and, thus, ignores the bulk of the important political and policy issues that arise in environmentalism.

5. Karl Marx, *Selected Writings*, ed. D. McLellan (London: Oxford University Press, 1977), 126.

6. August Comte, *Cathechisme positiviste* (Paris: Temple de l'humanite, 1957).

7. There are many who believe that when one construes human beings

as essential individual, this means that they are "individual through and through." Yet something that is essentially individual—that is, the nature of which is such that its individuality cannot be omitted from what it is—can also be elaborately involved with community, society, family, and other groups of individuals. It is, furthermore, an exaggeration to say that, to cite an anonymous commentator on an earlier version of these ideas, "life as studied by the life sciences is thoroughly social in nature with individual organisms embedded in interconnected supporting webs on which they are entirely dependent." Apart from the fact that being dependent on "supporting webs" does not render some being "thoroughly social"—so that, for example, the mere dependence of Rembrandt, George Elliot, Franz Liszt, Chekhov, and Virginia Wolff on innumerable social webs (economic, manufacturing, political, familiar, artistic, and so forth) by no means deprives them of the capacity to inject into their art a decisive individuality. For more on this, see Conway Zirkle, "Some Biological Aspects of Individualism," in *Essays on Individualism*, ed. F. Morley (Indianapolis: Liberty Press, 1977), 53–86. See also Theodosus Dobzhansky, *The Biological Basis of Human Freedom* (New York: Columbia University Press, 1956).

If, as has been argued by Roger W. Sperry, *Science and Moral Priority* (New York: Columbia University Press, 1983), human beings have a naturally grounded capacity for self-determination—that is, free will—it makes eminently good sense that they should become individuated in part depending on the extent and intensity of their choice to exercise their will. Their choices are then indeed their own, sovereign choices, not explainable without remainder by other aspects of their nature, including their social entanglements. This is in addition to their individuality as biological entities (such as with distinct fingerprints and other more or less unique attributes).

8. I draw here on an idea developed in Ayn Rand, "The Objectivist Ethics," in *The Virtue of Selfishness: A New Concept of Egoism* (New York: New American Library, 1961). See also Karl Popper, *Unending Quest* (Glasgow: Fontana/Collins, 1974), 194: "I think that values enter the world with life; and if there is life without consciousness (as I think there may well be, even in animals and man, for there appears to be such a thing as dreamless sleep) then, I suggest, there will also be objective values, even without consciousness." See also Tibor R. Machan, *Individuals and Their Rights* (LaSalle, Ill.: Open Court, 1989), chap. 2.

9. Of course, exactly what we should do in a precise case depends on the circumstances. If we encounter members of another species that clearly also possesses a moral nature, at least the potential would exist for peaceful collaboration between them and human beings on the basis of mutual recognition

of this common moral capacity. On the other hand, if this other species is a race of belligerent aliens from outer space intent on conquering and subjugating humanity, we might want to defeat them militarily before sitting down to discuss the ethics of the situation.

10. Bernard E. Rollin, *Animal Rights and Human Morality* (Buffalo, N.Y.: Prometheus, 1981), 14.

11. Rollin, *Animal Rights and Human Morality*, 14.

12. See a discussion of this in Mortimer Adler, *The Difference of Man and the Difference It Makes* (New York: World Publishing, 1968), 73 ff. See also Machan, *Individuals and Their Rights*. The former work concerns the issue of whether the human species is fundamentally distinct, the latter whether talk about "the nature of X" can have an objective foundation or must be nominal. On the latter, see Joel Wallman, *Aping Language* (New York: Cambridge University Press, 1992). Wallman argues that language is a uniquely human attribute and that these attempts establish nothing to contradict that fact. Compare Donald R. Griffin, *Animal Minds* (Chicago: University of Chicago Press, 1992). Griffin, on the other hand, argues that higher mentality is not unique to human beings, although he does not establish that any other animal aside from human beings is *uniquely dependent* on higher mental functions for the sustenance and flourishing of its life.

13. Adler, *The Difference of Man and the Difference It Makes*, 73.

14. Adler, *The Difference of Man and the Difference It Makes*, 73.

15. Adler, *The Difference of Man and the Difference It Makes*, 75.

16. The issue relating to the difference between human beings and other animals is not that of whether the former possess and the latter lack intelligence, although there is considerable difference of degree between the highest of adult primates and adult human beings. The issue is choice—free will or the capacity to initiate the specific human faculty of conceptual awareness of the world. It is this capacity that is vital to living a human life and, especially, to flourishing, something that other animals, though they may possess a minuscule measure of initiative, do not require for their lives and flourishing. On the pervasiveness of animal intelligence, see Eugene Linden, *The Octopus and the Orangutan* (New York: Dutton, 2002). For a comprehensive discussion of intelligence in humans and other animals, including a thorough bibliography and list of recommended readings, see Stephen Budiansky, *If a Lion Could Talk: Animal Intelligence and the Evolution of Consciousness* (New York: Free Press, 1998). It is, however, John R. Searle, in *Rationality in Action* (Cambridge, Mass.: MIT Press, 2001), who lays out the case of human choice most convincingly. Compare Craig Stanford, *Significant Others: The Ape-Human Continuum and the Quest for Human Nature* (New York: Basic, 2001).

17. There are those who admit of nuances here; Daniel Dennett, for example, has claimed that while fatalism is wrong, determinism is true but does not deprive us of choice—quite the contrary. This idea has been dubbed "soft -determinism," but it has its own set of problems because it fails to make room for the possibility of one choosing quite opposite from what one actually does choose. It makes room only for very complex, highly intelligent choices. See Daniel Dennett, *Freedom Evolves* (New York: Viking, 2003), and "Pulling Our Own Strings," an interview with Dennett in *Reason*, May 2003, 25–31.

18. For more, see Tibor R. Machan, *The Pseudo-Science of B. F. Skinner* (New Rochelle, N.Y.: Arlington House, 1974).

19. For more on this, see Robert Kane, *The Significance of Free Will* (London: Oxford University Press, 1998). For a thorough discussion of the idea of human agency—the capacity to act on one's own—see Edward Pols, *Acts of Our Being* (Boston: University of Massachusetts Press, 1982), and *Mind Regained* (Ithaca, N.Y.: Cornell University Press, 1998).

20. See Tibor R. Machan, "Applied Ethics and Free Will," *Journal of Applied Philosophy* 10 (1993): 59–72, and Tibor R. Machan, *Initiative—Human Agency and Society* (Stanford, Calif.: Hoover Institution Press, 2000).

21. For a position that denies this, see Daniel M. Wegner, *The Illusions of Conscious Will* (Cambridge, Mass.: MIT Press, 2002). Compare Benjamin Libet, Anthony Freedom, and Keith Sutherland, eds., *The Volitional Brain: Towards a Neuroscience of Free Will* (Thorverton, U.K.: Imprint Academic, 1999).

22. Tibor R. Machan, *Human Rights and Human Liberties* (Chicago: Nelson-Hall, 1975), and *Individuals and Their Rights*. See also Tibor R. Machan, "A Reconsideration of Natural Rights Theory," *American Philosophical Quarterly* 17 (1982): 61–72, and "Towards a Theory of Natural Individual Human Rights," *New Scholasticism* 61 (winter 1987): 33–78; "Are Human Rights Real?" *Review Journal of Philosophy and Social Science* 13 (1988): 1–22; and "Natural Rights Liberalism," *Philosophy and Theology* 4 (spring 1990): 253–65.

23. "Natural" in the sense of "part of what occurs in the world," versus "natural" as "in accordance with what kind of being something is," are related but not the same by any means. In the case of human beings, especially, the latter is something one has a choice to follow or try to circumvent (as when one fails to act as one's nature requires, say, rationally, generously).

24. A good example of the view on plants is Christopher Stone's *Should Trees Have Standing* (Palo Alto, Calif.: William Kaufmann, 1975). (Of course, everyone already agrees that trees *are* standing.) The animal rights case is pre-

sented most thoroughly by Tom Regan, *The Case for Animal Rights* (Berkeley: University of California Press, 1984). Not all antianthropocentricists are animal rights advocates, but most probably because they eschew the concept of rights altogether, not because they would draw a fundamental (morally and politically significant) distinction between other animals and human beings.

25. John Locke, *Two Treatises on Civil Government* (London: Everyman, 1698).

CHAPTER 3

1. There are some prominently featured and respectably published environmentalists, such as David M. Garaber, a scientist with the National Park Service, who, in reviewing Bill McKibben's *The End of Nature* (New York: Random House, 1989), say such things as, "Until such time as Homo sapiens should decide to rejoin nature, some of us can only hope for the right virus to come along" (*Los Angeles Times Book Review*, October 22, 1989, 9). McKibben, in turn, quotes with approval John Muir, the founder of the Sierra Club, who says, "Honorable representatives of the great saurians of older creation, may you long enjoy your lilies and rushes, and be blessed now and then with a mouthful of terror-stricken man by way of a dainty" (McKibben, *The End of Nature*, 176). Some of the more mainstream advocates of environmental reform advocate rather frightening policies concerning how human beings should understand their relationship to their environment. These include Jeremy Rifkin and Albert Gore, former vice president of the United States of America (who cannot be dismissed as some type of extremist not worth taking seriously). Their position is a more generalized version of that of D. W. Ehrenfeld in *The Arrogance of Humanism* (New York: Oxford University Press, 1978). This book regrets the capacity of human beings to manage parts of nature for their own ends (as if other animals didn't also do this as a matter of their life requirements). The idea seems to be that human beings ought to resign from life just because they have the capacity for making mistakes, for doing what is wrong. This view is excessively negative and indeed underestimates the sturdiness of the rest of nature.

2. Aristotle, Richard McKeon, ed., *The Basic Works of Aristotle* (*Politics* 1262a30–37) (New York: Random House, 1941), 1148.

3. The distinction between common end states and equally applicable procedures is made well in Robert Nozick, *Anarchy, State, and Utopia* (New York: Basic, 1974).

4. I should note here that some of these conclusions are still in dispute. Nevertheless, it is also fair to say that arguments made against the possibility of rational allocation of economic resources, the prudent use of the commons, and so forth are widely admitted to be telling. This is certainly not the place where we could decide the matter, let alone once and for all. I will assume, however, that enough trouble faces collectivist political systems, at least as far as fostering human productivity while avoiding having to conscript labor power is concerned, that drastic revisions would need to be made in order for them to become feasible, if they ever could be. The recent effort to develop what is called "market socialism" has run into serious theoretical difficulties. See, for example, David Schweickard, *Capitalism or Worker Control* (New York: Praeger, 1980); Julian Le Grand and Saul Estrin, eds., *Market Socialism* (New York: Clarendon, 1989); Ian Forbes, *Market Socialism* (London: Fabian Society, 1986); David Miller, *Market, State, and Community: Theoretical Foundations of Market Socialism* (New York: Oxford University Press, 1989); James A. Yunker, *Socialism Revised and Modernized: The Case for Pragmatic Market Socialism* (New York: Praeger, 1992); and Anders Aslund, *Market Socialism or the Restoration of Capitalism?* (New York: Cambridge University Press, 1992). See, however, Anthony De Jasay, *Market Socialism: A Scrutiny "This Square Circle"* (London: Institute of Economic Affairs, 1990), and N. Scott Arnold, *The Political Philosophy of Market Socialism* (London: Oxford University Press, 1994).

5. Garrett Hardin, "The Tragedy of the Commons," in *Pollution, Resources, and the Environment*, ed. Alain C. Enthoven and A. Myrick Freeman III (New York: Norton, 1973), 5.

6. Robert Heilbroner, "After Communism," *The New Yorker*, September 10, 1990, 92.

7. Heilbroner, "After Communism," 99.

8. Heilbroner, "After Communism," 100.

9. In other words, a feasible political system must focus on prohibitions, enforced by officers of the law, rather than on outcomes. For a good discussion of this point—contrasting end-state and procedural features of a political order—see Robert Nozick, *Anarchy, State, and Utopia* (New York: Basic, 1974).

10. For more on this, see Tibor R. Machan, "Terrorism and Objective Moral Principles," *International Journal of World Peace* 4, no. 4 (October–December 1987): 31–40.

11. Garrett Hardin, "The Tragedy of the Commons," *Science*, December 13, 1968, 1244.

12. The point can be made rather simply via personal relations. Force is

justified in self-defense or defending someone who has been attacked and has asked to be helped. As a means of problem solving, however, force is at best an emergency measure—as when one strikes a friend who is hysterical—but not as a steady policy.

13. It is important to stress that in proposing this libertarian approach, no promise of full satisfaction is being offered. The perfect is, after all, the enemy of the good! There are some risks with every system, including one in which individuals have the full right to gain and keep holdings and to unite in their disposition of these holdings. However, such a relatively decentralized system does not officially permit the deployment of government powers to favor any holder over others. Not that corruption cannot occur, but compared to the kind of corruption of massive collectivist systems, such as socialism and communism, the risks of abuse and mismanagement are relatively minor. For more, see Tibor R. Machan, "Reflections on the Right to Private Property," *Journal des Economists et des Estudes Humaines* 11 (March 2000): 179–95. For an extensive exploration of the theory of individual rights, which some environmentalist scoff at in their effort to secure for government nearly unlimited powers to regiment resource usage, see Tibor R. Machan, *Individuals and Their Rights* (LaSalle, Ill.: Open Court, 1989).

14. This is Bastiat's famous 1850 essay "What Is Seen and What Is Not Seen," in *Selected Essays on Political Economy*, ed. George B. de Huszar (Irvington-on-Hudson, N.Y.: Foundation for Economic Education, 1995), 1–50, in which he shows that one of the problems in disputing the merits of state action is that what is displaced by it is not visible, whereas what it achieves can be pointed to easily. (Thus, a tax may lead to the building of a widely observed public park but deprive someone of the ability to purchase new tires for a car and may even cause a fatal crash, but no one will ever know.)

15. For one account of the results of the TVA project, see Michael J. McDonald and John Muldowny, *TVA and the Dispossessed: The Resettlement of Population in the Norris Dam Area* (Nashville: University of Tennessee Press, 1982).

16. For a history of this system, see Peter H. Salus, *Casting the Net: From ARPANET to Internet and Beyond* (New York: Addison Wesley Longman, 1995).

17. For an account, see David Burke, *Road through the Wilderness: The Story of the Transcontinental Railway* (New York: International Specialized Book Services, 2001).

18. See Jim Lehrer's interview with Gunn at the PBS website, www.pbs. org/newshour/bb/transportation/jan-june02/gunn_6–13.html.

19. Terry L. Anderson and Donald R. Leal, "Nature's Entrepreneurs," *The Freeman* 48 (November 1998): 647.

20. For more on this, see Tibor R. Machan, *Classical Individualism* (London: Routledge, 1998).

21. See Terry L. Anderson and Donald R. Leal, *Enviro-Capitalists: Doing Good while Doing Well* (Lanham, Md.: Rowman & Littlefield, 1998).

22. This approach is actually being taken, here and there, by the U.S. State Department, the World Bank, and the International Monetary Fund vis-à-vis countries asking for financial support for various projects. Conditions, such as extensive selling off of state property and privatization, are laid down that need to be met prior to the granting of support.

CHAPTER 4

1. Tibor R. Machan, *Human Rights and Human Liberties* (Chicago: Nelson-Hall, 1975), 202–3.

2. Tibor R. Machan, "Some Doubts about Animal Rights," *Journal of Value Inquiry* 19 (1985): 73–75; "Do Animals Have Rights?" *Public Affairs Quarterly* 5 (April 1991): 163–73; and "Why Human Beings May Use Animals," *Journal of Value Inquiry* 36 (2002): 9–14.

3. Peter Singer (quoting his essay "Animal Liberation," *New York Review of Books*, April 5, 1973, 17), in "Animal Liberation at 30," *New York Review of Books* 50, no. 8 (May 15, 2003): 26.

4. Singer, "Animal Liberation at 30," 26.

5. W. G. Maclagan, "Self and Others: A Defense of Altruism," *Philosophical Quarterly* 4 (1954): 109–10.

6. Quoted in *The Week*, November 16, 2002, 19.

INDEX

131

ABOUT THE AUTHOR

Tibor R. Machan, who was smuggled out of Hungary at age fourteen, is professor emeritus of philosophy at Auburn University and currently Distinguished Fellow and Freedom Communications Professor of Business Ethics and Free Enterprise at the Argyros School of Business & Economics at Chapman University. He is a research fellow at the Hoover Institution at Stanford University. He is a syndicated and freelance columnist, author of more than twenty-five books, most recently *The Passion for Liberty* (Rowman & Littlefield, 2003), and editor of seventeen others. He has written more than one hundred scholarly papers. He was visiting professor at the U.S. Military Academy, West Point between 1992 and 1993. He was editor of *Reason Papers*, an annual journal of interdisciplinary normative studies, for twenty-five years. He lectures in Europe, South Africa, New Zealand, and Latin America on business ethics and political philosophy. Machan lives in Silverado, California, with Erin, his younger daughter.

Studies in Social, Political, and Legal Philosophy
Series Editor: James P. Sterba, University of Notre Dame

This series analyzes and evaluates critically the major political, social, and legal ideals, institutions, and practices of our time. The analysis may be historical or problem-centered; the evaluation may focus on theoretical underpinnings or practical implications. Among the recent titles in the series are: